THE BROKEN TREE

THE BROKEN TREE

A personal memoir of a search for family

Anita Venes

Matador
9 Priory Business Park,
Wistow Road, Kibworth Beauchamp,
Leicestershire. LE8 0RX
Tel: 0116 279 2299
Email: books@troubador.co.uk
Web: www.troubador.co.uk/matador
Twitter: @matadorbooks

ISBN 978 183859 247 9

British Library Cataloguing in Publication Data.
A catalogue record for this book is available from the British Library.

Printed and bound by CPI Group (UK) Ltd, Croydon, CR0 4YY
Typeset in 11pt Adobe Garamond Pro by Troubador Publishing Ltd, Leicester, UK

Matador is an imprint of Troubador Publishing Ltd

Dedicated to Shaun and David
for their love and understanding.

Contents

Preface

MANY PEOPLE – FRIENDS AND FAMILY, AND THOSE WHOM I
have known and worked with – have encouraged me to write about
my experiences. This book is about a search for answers.

I have had a long and interesting life, consisting of a traumatic
childhood followed by a wonderfully rewarding career – two careers,
in fact. I have discovered much of my family history along the way,
but many memories were lost to me over my lifetime. I much regret
that I was unable to ask my parents about their lives and the reasons
behind some of the things that happened to me.

I am lucky to have two loving sons, whose successes in their
lives give me so much pleasure. They do not know all of this
story because, over the years, I have found it difficult to begin to
tell them. This book is for Shaun and David, for their love and
understanding. I am grateful to my husband John for his love and
support throughout the writing of this memoir. I have the huge joy
of being a grandmother to our four bright grandchildren – Dylan,
Abigail, William and Natty. My story is also for them, so that they
may know their history.

My book is also dedicated to my complex, funny, loving sister,
Sandra, who has come through so much heartache to be reconciled
to all that happened to her. We are now enjoying the happiest times

together. Thanks to my brother Graham and Pat for the joy they have brought to us, and to all my nephews and nieces and all the members of our complicated family tree, thank you for your love, friendship and support.

Anita Elwell

2019

THE VENES FAMILY TREE

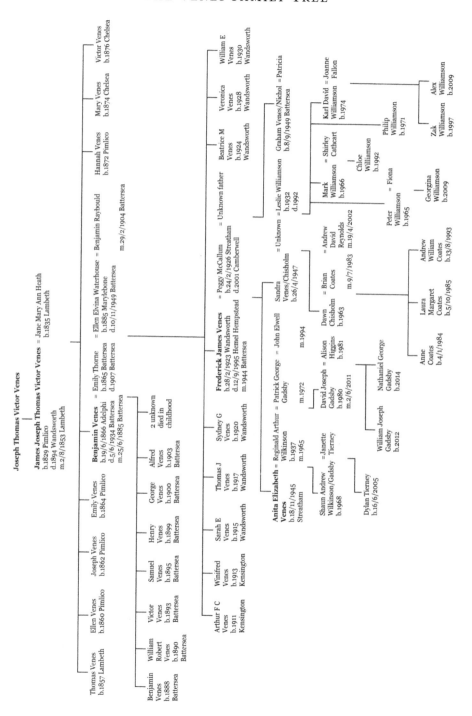

The McCallum Family Tree

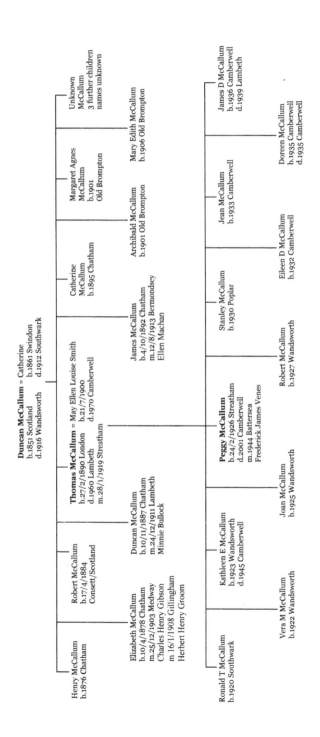

Part One

CHAPTER ONE

Who Am I?

"You've talked a lot about your mother; tell me about your father?"

"I never had a father," I declared.

There was a long pause.

"That's strange, Anita; how did that come about?" my therapist continued.

"Well, I mean I never met my father and I don't know anything about him. I was put into a children's home when I was three, along with my baby sister," I explained.

"So, you probably spent three years living with him before that time?"

"I suppose I did."

"Did you never wonder why he gave you away? Why he never came to find you? Why he didn't love you?"

At these words, I fell apart. All the loneliness, hurt and longing of my early years – all that I had suppressed and forgotten – came flooding back to me. I felt an overwhelming surge of pain, anguish and loss as my therapist said these words. I cried for a long while.

In the following silence, I said, "I never thought about him in that way; well, actually, I never thought about him at all. I must have pushed those events to the back of my mind. I was too small to ask questions."

Suddenly, a scenario occurred to me about the day I was taken away from my parents: *What did I do wrong? How did that happen? Did my dad or my mum or both of them contact The Children's Society to ask them to take my baby, sister, Sandra, and me away? Why? Did I cry and struggle, or did I meekly hold the stranger's hand and walk away? Children of three are very attached to their parents and familiar people, and can declare what they want – loudly. Did I object that day?*

The only memory I have of my father was of once climbing up a dark staircase and standing on a narrow landing by a door, and my father – having struggled up the stairs, with my sister in a pram – said to me, "Don't let go of the pram; hold tight, there's a good girl."

He disappeared through a door. I looked back at the long staircase and was afraid of falling down. I have no other memories of him. I never saw him again.

———❀———

During 1986, in the weeks following counselling, long-forgotten snatches of memories would flash into my mind without warning, many of them very painful and with more questions: *What happened? Where were you? Why didn't you want us?*

All my life, I have had huge problems with loss, particularly with an irrational fear of losing people and of being alone. I had a sense of not being worthy of love from anyone; I was very angry inside about lots of things and felt unable to rationalise those emotions. I began to understand, for the first time, where those feelings might stem from. I knew I would have to explore this turbulent past to find answers before I could move forward. My mind was in turmoil as I tried to carry on as normal.

I began receiving counselling support when I was forty-one and at a very low point in my life. I was stressed, overworked and lonely, with a failing marriage. I needed to find a way out of the hole I was in, to unburden myself from all the thoughts that kept me awake at night, and were leading to bad judgements at work and neglect of my family's needs. Those questions about my parents were unexpected, but they opened the floodgates.

"Why don't you try to find him?" my therapist asked.

"I wouldn't know where to start. He might be dead. He might not want to know me," I stated.

As part of my therapy, I was encouraged to take positive steps to take control and begin to understand my past. I began by taking a trip back to the local children's home where my baby sister and I had been placed for a while. I was able to wander around picking up memories. The manager of the home showed me records in which details of my sister's and my stay there were listed. It had a strange effect on me, as it confirmed, for the first time, that I had actually lived there. The house had recently become a home for disturbed teenagers and one of them asked me why I was there.

When I told her, she remarked, "Why would you want to visit this place again?"

My answer seemed to surprise her, and she started to tell me her own sad story.

In 1986, I made a trip on my own to St Catherine's House in London, where births, marriages and deaths were then registered. I was shown how to look through the huge ledgers to search for my father's name. I failed in my attempts to find out anything about him and became resigned to the thought that it would never happen. I did, however, learn from my mother's record that she had another child in 1949, a boy named Graham. He had been adopted at birth.

This is my story, as I now know it.

I was born in my mother's family home, at Sulina Road, Streatham Hill, South East London on 18th November 1945, just a week after Armistice Day. My mother's maiden name was Peggy McCallum. She had married my father, Frederick James Venes, in August 1944, and they went to live with his family. They later moved in with his brother,

Charles, and lodged subsequently with my mum's parents before, finally, moving to a rented room in a house owned by a Mr D in 1948. This accommodation was very basic, with little furniture. My parents were never happy there.

My grandparents' house was an old, terraced cottage rented by my grandmother, Ellen. It was small and overcrowded. Living there were my mother and father, my grandparents, and several of my mother's brothers and sisters, my baby sister and me. I was baptised on 6th January 1946, when I was less than two months old, at All Saints' Church in Brixton.

The part of war-torn London where I was born had been heavily bombed during the Blitz. There were, and still are, large properties with wealthy owners in the district, but also a lot of poor, run-down properties. Food was short due to strict rationing. Jobs were hard to come by. Daily life was a struggle to make ends meet. My mother was nineteen when I was born, and my sister, Sandra, arrived seventeen months later, further adding to the overcrowded household. Two of my mother's sisters developed tuberculosis (TB) and died from it. There was great concern for us babies in the house. We were cared for by the extended family and, apparently, thrived on the love and affection of them all. One of my mother's sisters, Eileen, once told me that she used to spend time looking after us and taking us to a nearby sweet shop.

Thomas McCallum, my mother's father, was known as a hard-drinking and sometimes violent man; he was born in Lambeth in 1890. In 1919, he married May Ellen Louise Plummer, who was already a widow at twenty – her first husband having been killed just five months before, in his first weeks as a gunner in the First World War.

When they married, Thomas was in the merchant navy; he worked on four ships from 1919 to 1921. His last ship, the SS *Estrellano* was sunk later by a German submarine. He was described as a fireman and a trimmer.

A fireman's work involved shovelling coal into the boilers in the ship's bowels, and maintaining the fires. Once the furnaces had been fed, the fire had to be kept going throughout his watch, so that all the coal burned efficiently. This involved a lot of work close to the open flames. Feeding the furnaces, with their insatiable appetite for coal, was a physically demanding and exhausting job. He would be working in a very dusty, smoky environment at temperatures around 100°F.

Trimmers would move coal from one area in the bunkers to the next, in order to maintain a constant supply of fuel at the bunker doors. The trimmers also saw to it that a pile of coal was always at the ready at each fireman's feet. They also had to be sure that the piles of coal were adjusted evenly or 'trimmed', which is where their name came from. Trimmers were even lower in social status than the men they served. Theirs was the dirtiest, most physically demanding and dangerous job on the ship. They received the lowest pay. Thomas's father (Duncan) and four of Thomas's brothers also worked as labourers on ships. There was a Duncan McCallum in each of three generations: all hard men and all alcoholics. They were known locally as the 'Mad Macs'. Thomas once sent home money to May, his mother, knowing his father drank away the family income. Duncan seized this money for drink. When Thomas returned, he and his father had a terrible fight, and Thomas never spoke to him again.

I know that my own father learned a trade in painting and decorating at some point. He next found work as a lathe hand in a factory, but work was irregular and he got into debt. My dad left my mum in August 1948, but he continued to maintain us all financially for a while. By 1950, he had lost contact with us.

The owner of the house my mum was renting began to pester my mother when his wife was in hospital and, eventually, she gave in to his demands. When she realised she was pregnant, he refused to believe he was the father. My mother had to leave her job and was then not supported financially by either my father or Mr D – the father of the baby. She was sent away to a nursing home to have the baby, who was born on 9th September 1949 and named Graham. Mum went from hospital back to her own parents' home and she found work at a Sainsbury's store. It is clear that Peggy's family could not continue to give shelter to all of us and another baby. My brother was placed immediately in foster care and he was adopted in August 1950. My mother never saw him again and never spoke to anyone about him.

There were problems over money and looking after two small children. One of my mother's brothers, who was living with them at the time, said that we were so poor that there were no bedclothes for us two babies and we had to be covered with old clothing at night to keep us warm. Subsequently, Mum was forced to leave her job and her parents' house. Sharing the news of an illegitimate pregnancy with her husband and her family must have been difficult for her because of the huge stigma associated with illegitimacy in those days. This news seems to have been the last straw for my father and for her parents.

My father returned to live with his parents, and we infants lived in our paternal grandparents' household for some time. My mother must have been able to visit us, although she was not reconciled with her husband. I have learned that, for a short time, my sister Sandra and I were briefly fostered, together with our new baby brother, Graham, prior to his adoption.

My father got into trouble over some petty car crime, and was imprisoned for a short sentence. Whilst he was away, tragically, his mother died. Subsequently, in July 1949, my sister and I were placed at St Mary's Nursery, Cheam, Surrey, in the care of the Church of England Children's Society (formerly called the Waifs and Strays Society, and now The Children's Society), which would continue to have responsibility for my care for the rest of my childhood.

Clearly, my mother was aware of the decision to put us 'in care', but was not around to see us go. Many years later, I heard that she visited the offices of The Children's Society regularly after we were placed in a children's home, asking for news of us. I cannot know if the mental problems that my mother suffered from for most of her adult life began at this time. I can only imagine that it was a very dark time for her, as she was totally unsupported by her family, had very little money, and was required to pay her family allowance directly to The Children's Society for the care of Sandra and me. She needed to find work and a place to live. She lost contact with all her children.

When my sister and I were together at the nursery, I can recall sitting under a tree with someone called 'Nurse'. The tree was a large horse chestnut. It was approaching autumn, and huge leaves were falling. I can feel my delight at this and remember that the nurse sat with me on her knee and showed me how to strip the flesh from the leaf to leave a skeleton. I have a vivid memory of that moment. I also recall the ritual when all the children had to line up each morning to receive a dose of cod liver oil, despite some protests.

At age four, a report from the children's home in Cheam describes me as "A dear sensitive little girl, she has a charming manner and is beautifully spoken. She likes to help and is very capable, she is of average intelligence."

One day a nurse said to me, "Come along, we must tidy you up; your mother is coming to see you."

I was lifted up onto a cold surface, and my face, knees and hands were scrubbed. I was dressed in smart, clean clothes. I recall I cried in protest and was scolded.

I can visualise my mother walking up the drive as I stood with a nurse at the front door. She was with a man, who was shorter than her, and they both greeted me with smiles. She asked me if I had been a good girl – a question that was put to me many times during my early years. I suspect it was a reflection of my lively personality.

A report written in 1949 by the Children's Society about Sandra, me and our mother says, "There is a very strong bond of love between her and the children, it is going to be very difficult for them to let someone else replace their mother."

I did not see my mother again until many years had passed, and I buried any memories I had of her.

CHAPTER TWO

A Long Way Away

ONE DAY, IN JULY 1949, MY BABY SISTER AND I WERE PUT into a black taxicab for a long and final journey away from London and all that we knew. I remember kneeling up in the cab and being told to wave to everybody. We left the children's home and travelled by train to Derbyshire to one of The Children's Society's Homes, which had space for both of us to stay together. My mother had begged the authorities not to send us so far away, as she would not be able to afford the fare to come to see us. We were transferred to the children's home called Eaton Hill (the Home), in a village called Little Eaton a few miles from Derby. Each time we were moved, no one ever told us or explained to us what was happening, nor where everyone we had known had disappeared to. Children were not expected to ask questions and answers would be minimal: "Sit still!"; "Don't ask questions!"; and " Hold your tongue." (How do you do that?)

Not knowing any details about my past has been the hardest thing to come to terms with all my life and has made me very anxious about change. All my early childhood memories were buried, and I forgot everything and everyone I had known. These thoughts have saddened me when I now look at our precious grandsons and our beautiful granddaughter – who are much loved by their families and so familiar with everything around them. I am very glad that they have such wonderful parents and a secure and happy homelife.

Although my mother never saw us again whilst we were children, she kept in touch with The Children's Society to learn where we were and how we were doing. During the years I was in foster care, she wrote letters to me, which, sadly, I neither saw nor knew about. My foster mother decided they would unsettle me.

Many years later, when I asked The Children's Society for information about my early years, I received copies of correspondence from my mother to The Children's Society that show how much she wanted to keep in touch with my sister and me. It appears that she made several attempts to visit us and, sadly, was unable to do so. She reveals in later correspondence that she had received no financial support from my father, yet she was sending money and gifts for the two of us at the Home, which must have been extraordinarily hard for her. Her eloquent letters show a deep concern for our welfare and a great sense of loss when we were moved so far away. She feared that we would forget all about her, and, sadly, we did. Some of the correspondence shows her concern and love for us despite the distance between us, and the ways she tried to keep herself in our memories.

This is a letter from my mother, dated 14th July 1951, to Mrs Lomas, housemother at Eaton Hill Children's Home, Little Eaton, Derbyshire:

Just a few lines hoping that the children are well, I have been a bit worried as I haven't heard from you, that is why I am late in writing as I was waiting to see when would be the best time to come up to see them, as I know you said Anita will be going away.

I am enclosing the children's Postal Orders, I send them

separate ones now as I thought that they would like to feel independent and have one each as I remember when they were both very small how I used to give them their sweet money and didn't they love to hear a couple of pennies rattle in their pockets.

Well Mrs Lomas I do hope that nothing is amiss, and also that the children liked the snaps also their cards. Please give them my love and a big kiss for me. When you write would you please send me the size of their shoes and also the size of their socks, and tell Anita that I will bring her some writing books up and some picture books for Sandra, do you think they would like some paints and painting books or have they got these? Please let me know as soon as possible as I want to get something each week before my holidays.

I will say goodbye now, hoping to hear from you soon and also that you are keeping fit and well. Cheerio for now, all my love to Anita and Sandra.

Yours sincerely Mrs P Venes

In a later letter to The Children's Society, my mother writes the following:

I wonder if you could advise me whether it would be possible for me to have the children adopted, please. Don't think that this is a sudden impulse on my behalf, for I have thought it well over in my mind and I think that it will be the only way they will ever have any future, and although it will be heart-breaking for me to have to part with them. I should be more contented in my mind if I thought they were having the love and care that means so much to children. So, Miss R., if you could advise me on this at all I should be very grateful.

The following is taken from a letter from one of The Children's Society's workers to their head office, regarding Mrs Peggy Venes,

Anita E Venes (born 18th November 1945), Sandra Venes (born 26th April 1947) and Graham Venes (born 8th September 1949):

Thank you very much for your letter of February 1st and for kindly letting me have the one you received from Mrs Venes concerning the future of her children. It does seem a very sad state of affairs that she should want all the children adopted. It is Especially sad, I think, that she should consider having the little girls of her marriage adopted.

As you rightly point out it would be very difficult for the adoption of Anita and Sandra to be arranged without the consent of Mr Venes. Do you think there is any chance of his whereabouts being located? As Graham is an illegitimate child she has had the least of all to do with him.

We have talked to the matron of our Cheam Branch about Anita and Sandra both are intelligent little girls, very fond of each other and of their mother who visits them when she is able. If the two little girls are to be adopted I think it would be best if Mrs Venes should fade out of the picture for everyone's sake, although this will be a very painful thing for her to do. I gather that Mrs Venes is a very poor type of woman and one can understand that the chances of her being able to make a home for her two children are rather slender. As however, there is a very strong bond of love between her and the children, it is going to be difficult for them to let someone else replace their mother. Adoption for the little boy, on the other hand, would appear to be the most sensible arrangement.

Thus was our future life decided for us – and for our mother. I feel so sad to know that there was no way she could get help to keep us together, as her own parents had given up on her and us. Although our maternal grandparents lived on into the 1970s, we never heard mention of them at all. I have found a photograph of the two of them sitting on a park bench. My grandmother's face is the image of my own now that I am older.

Here is a letter from my mother to Mrs Parnell (deputy houseparent) dated 9th August 1951:

First let me introduce myself to you, this is Mrs Venes, Anita and Sandra's mother writing to you. I received a letter and also a card from Mrs Lomas telling me that the children would be going away before I start my holidays, I was very disappointed at not being able to come and see them, as it has been such a long time and I have been looking forward to coming for weeks but I am pleased to think that they are having such a lovely holiday and I do hope that they both enjoy themselves. Would you please ask Mrs Lomas to let me know when they will be back again then I can arrange to come later on; I will say goodnight now hoping that the children are well and happy.

Yours sincerely Mrs P Venes

This must have been an extremely anxious and sad time for her, as she came to realise that her links with us were fast disappearing. She was never able to travel to see either of us.

A letter from my mother to Mrs Lomas at Eaton Hill Children's Home, dated 3rd September 1951:

I have had to write to you as I have been wondering how the children are. It seems such a long time since I saw them that I am afraid they will forget me. I was very disappointed at not being able to see them on my holidays but all the same I hope they enjoyed themselves also I hope that you had a nice holiday. I hope Anita is getting on alright at school, please tell them both that I am very sorry about not being able to come to see them but hope there will be another opportunity in the near future, as I would love to see how much they have grown.

I am sorry to worry you like this but I feel so very upset just lately; it wasn't so hard when I thought I would be seeing them, but now it seems as though I am completely forgotten to them, and I am sure they must wonder why I did not come up there.

I will not take up any more of your time now Mrs Lomas. I just want to send all my love and kisses to the children and God bless them. Goodnight, I am hoping that you are keeping well.

Yours sincerely Mrs P Venes

PS I will send them some money the next time I write.

There is a further postscript from Mrs Lomas to head office, which says, "Just received this, have not answered; please advise me, if you think I should."

The following is a letter from my mother to the Waifs and Strays Society, dated 23rd September 1951:

Dear Sir, Thank you very much for the letter about my two daughters and also the photograph of Sandra. I was rather surprised to hear that they had been fostered out, and I do hope that they are well cared for as I am really a bit worried as one reads about so many terrible things happening to children these days.

I would very much like to visit them but if they are in Wales, which I believe is where they went for their holidays, there is little chance that I shall be able to get there in one day to see them. Perhaps you would keep me informed on their progress and welfare from time to time and if I can any time arrange to see them I would very much like to. I would also like to send them something now and again, for I have been sending them some sweet money which I believe they have been saving up. It is Anita's birthday soon and I have been saving a few shillings to buy her something, so if when the time comes you would let me know who to forward anything on to, I would be very grateful. I will draw to a close now, hoping that my two little girls are very happy, and thank you for writing.

Yours sincerely Mrs P Veness

The true pain and loss my mother felt when she wrote this heartrending letter is very much apparent. It is possible that the mental health problems that she suffered from for the rest of her life stemmed from this time, as she began to realise that all her children were lost to her. It seems incredible that she was not consulted about the fostering, nor was there any help available for her to be able to visit us. The Children's Society appears to have taken a decision to distance my mother from the possibility of seeing us again, even though we were still small children. The following letter suggests my mother was coming to terms with the inevitable adoption of my sister, from whom I was then separated.

A letter to Miss Laurie, Social Worker for The Children's Society sent by my mother on 7th November 1952:

Dear Miss Laurie,

I am sorry I have been so long in writing to you but I have been attending the hospital with my nerves and also I have a goitre forming in my neck, which I'll have to have operated on as soon as there is a bed in the hospital for me, well I have waited up till now before writing to you about Sandra in case they sent for me to go in for my operation but have not heard anything so far, so under the circumstances I can't say anything as regard to Sandra as I don't know how long it will be before I go into hospital.

I don't know if you have heard any more about a home for Sandra but I would be very much grateful to you if you could get her settled for me, as the doctor said he would like me to go away for a few weeks after my operation as my nerves are in a very bad state. I have thought things over and I don't think it would be fair to Sandra to have her home for a few days and then send her back again not knowing when she may return to us, it is not only accommodation that stands in the way, it is also my health, so if you can find a home for her I would be very grateful and happy to know that she is happy.

I am really very sorry and disappointed over not being able to have her with me but it is far better to be sensible about an affair like this than to make promises that may have to be broken. So, Miss Laurie, I hope you will understand and write and let me know what you decide. There is just one other request: would you please let me have Sandra's address as I would like to send her something for Christmas. I will close now thanking you once again.

Yours sincerely

Mrs P Payne

This previous letter was written when Sandra was five and a half – on the date of my seventh birthday. My mother remarried in 1953. Payne was her new surname.

The houseparents of the Home were good, kind people; we called them Uncle Don and Aunty Sheila. He was a tall, quietly spoken, gentle person who took pains to get to know each of us and to show us that we were cared about. He played the cello in the local chamber orchestra, and the lovely music often filled the house after we were tucked up in bed. It was a happy coincidence that I later took up lessons on the cello, which became a lifelong joy to me. I have a few memories of my time there, mostly of being naughty and sent to bed early. I once put my sister inside the grandfather clock in the entrance hall and closed the door. Her squeals brought trouble on my head. I was a lively, talkative child and settled quickly into the new home.

I started school in the village whilst at the Home. I remember taking a long walk across fields and a main road each day to get to the little, brick Victorian building. I remember trying on the communal shoes in the Home's boot room, and struggling with black plimsolls that were too big for me. Someone sewed black elastic across the tops of the shoes so they would stay on. The village children could identify us as the 'Home kids' from these small indignities. In winter, the classroom had an open coal fire with a guard around to keep children safe from it. The caretaker would pop in with a bucketful of coke at intervals during the lessons and stoke the embers. I had a strong cockney accent apparently, and this caused some confusion amongst the teachers and pupils alike. The quiet ordered life of the Home was a haven for me, and I can recall playing in large gardens; seeing a rope swing, which the boys would not share; and trudging across the fields full of scary cows and, sometimes, sheep with lambs.

One evening after tea, as we little ones were taken upstairs to prepare for bed, a couple arrived in the hall below. I seem to recall a conversation about a girl who had gone home to Birmingham for the weekend and that the couple had come to take her out for the day, as they had done before. I guess this conversation was repeated in front of me when I was older. What I do know is that just as Nurse had put on my pyjamas and was cleaning my teeth, she was called to bring me down to the houseparents' drawing room, a place out of bounds to the children normally. She hurried down, with me in my pyjamas, only to be told that the couple were to take me out for the weekend and I had to be dressed again; it was very confusing for a little child. In the drawing room stood a man and a woman, and they looked me up and down. They were being encouraged to take my sister and I out for the weekend. They clearly thought that two of us together would be a handful, so I was chosen. It was quite exciting to be dressed again and to go out in the dark. I was bundled into their car, and off we went.

I can't remember the details, but I know that the girl I replaced that evening was called Shirley and that the couple lived in a village that was also called Shirley. It was a car journey of about fifteen miles, with me asleep in the back, which took a considerable time in those days. I was lifted out of the car, and taken into a cottage and up to a bedroom with a large double bed. It seemed enormous to me, and it had no familiar cot sides to keep me in. I was shown a chamber pot under the bed, which was to be used in the night if I wanted to wee. There were so many new and puzzling experiences. There were no explanations given as to where I was, who these new people were or how long I was going to stay there.

Subsequently, I visited their home for the weekend on several occasions, and enjoyed the new experience. I recall that whenever they took me back to the Home I refused to get out of the car, clinging to the seats and screaming my head off. It was not understood at the time that the trauma of leaving my family and then London had started a profound reaction in me to being taken away from my 'base' and in coping with new situations. A fear of losing people would haunt me all my life as a result of those early experiences. This persuaded The Children's Society that it would be advantageous to me to live with the couple, and, eventually, they decided to foster me full-time. My little sister was left behind for the time being.

CHAPTER THREE

Village Life

DORIS AND TOM, THE FOSTER PARENTS I WENT TO LIVE with, had no children of their own. I never discovered why, and their relationship was anything but close throughout my childhood, and I was to experience much unhappiness and, eventually, the total breakdown of their marriage during the years I spent with them. Doris was a strong, dominant woman, who was not tall but well built. She had an outgoing, sociable personality and a quick temper. She was the oldest of three children, with two brothers: one living in the next village and one a few miles away. They had lost their mother to diphtheria when Doris was a small child, and she was raised by her aunt in the village. Her father was a haulage contractor who, in my time with the family, was living and working in a village some distance away in the Derbyshire Dales. I remember well a sepia portrait of her mother, which hung on a wall in the cottage – she was an attractive Edwardian lady in high-necked lace blouse, with rows of pearls and her hair tucked neatly under in a bun. She had a serene but serious expression on her face. She was never talked about.

Doris's experiences of being mothered were fractured too. I have no doubt that her methods of caring for me reflected her own upbringing. There were many phrases often heard in households in those days that were commonly applied to me by her.

Firstly, there was "Children should be seen and not heard", which was a command I heard frequently, but found difficult to obey. In practice, it meant not interrupting when an adult was speaking, being silent at the table, no arguing, no rudeness, no fidgeting, obeying instructions without comment, not venturing an opinion and many other rules that it was so easy to forget. Imagine that around the table at mealtimes these days!

Then there was "Spare the rod and spoil the child" and "She needs a good hiding". These translated into me receiving a hard, physical response to any misdemeanour. Smacking children as punishment was common and recommended to "knock the wickedness out of them". As I grew, the hand smack became a leather belt. Unruly, badly behaved children were thought to be a reflection on a family's 'good name'.

Another phrase was "Manners maketh man". This proved to be a very worthwhile lesson since I have always been able to mix with all kinds of people and taught my own children to know how to behave appropriately in social situations. However, I was nagged constantly about my manners at home, and when out and about: "Sit up straight"; "Elbows off the table"; and "Mind your Ps and Qs" (whatever they were). There was such a lot to remember.

Doris had a great sense of duty and a moral obligation to bring me up as a decent, well-behaved, Christian soul. I think there was a belief that a child coming from a 'broken home' automatically would be unruly, and therefore had to be chastised and tamed. The Children's Society expected that I would be brought up in a good Christian environment, and the local vicar was charged with some oversight of my attendance at church and conduct, together with the school teacher who also reported on me on a regular basis to The Children's Society's social worker. The fact that I was a bewildered little girl needing only to be loved was simply not understood.

Many people then believed that to praise a child was to make her or him conceited and boastful. Success was acknowledged only grudgingly. In my foster home, love was never spoken out loud and certainly not in company. When we met Doris's friends in the street she would say, "She's not ours, you know."

I used to wonder who I belonged to. Doris had no sense of being loving. I was never cuddled as I recall, and, when naughty, I was constantly threatened with, "We'll send you back to the home for bad girls." I had no idea as a little girl what that meant, but it sounded too dreadful to risk.

I developed facial tics and grimaces, and was described as "nervy and highly strung". I can now see this must have been as a result of the many sudden changes in my early years and the lack of love. It is well known now that a lack of love and 'attachment' in early childhood causes significant problems in later life; I can vouch for that. I was always lonely and anxious about what might happen to me.

Although I couldn't express how I felt, my childhood was characterised by a sense of bewilderment; all I wanted was to be loved; but I never felt that. Here and there around the village, I would catch a glimpse of family love – a mother's hug, a child's smile, praise or a closeness that was never mine – it always out of reach, denied to me.

Doris was very attached to her father, and, although he was not living close by, she saw him regularly. She was devastated at his death when I was still a small child. He had supported her financially, paid for extensive improvements to the cottage, and provided for the holidays we used to enjoy for a few years in Scarborough or Llandudno, with him and his second wife. All the extended family would join together for a holiday. When he died, his will left his wealth largely to his widow – a fact Doris never got over. She was thus poorer financially, and turned on Tom for his lack of ambition and drive.

Tom was a quiet, solitary figure in my childhood, moving about the house like a shadow, trying to avoid confrontation with his wife as often as possible.

⸻

I started school, again, at the even smaller village school in Shirley. It had one schoolroom for children of all ages from five to eleven years old, and one teacher, the headmistress. There were about a dozen children at the school then. The teacher was an elderly lady, near retirement age, who lived in the adjoining school house. A door with a little window in it, covered by a curtain, led into her living room. Each morning, she would set us tasks to do and threaten us with dire consequences if we moved or spoke whilst she went into her house for a cup of tea. We would watch for a twitch of the little curtain, which meant she was keeping an eye on us.

I was encouraged to call my foster mother 'Aunty Doris'. Any friends of theirs were to be addressed as 'aunty' and 'uncle'. Aunty Doris had decided that she did not like my first name, Anita, due to it being, she said, "A foreign sort of name." She decided I would be called Ann. Furthermore, she also disliked my surname, which was Venes, so she decided she would change it to theirs, which was Shepherd. So, I became known as Ann Shepherd. I was not consulted about any of this.

One day, the teacher was testing our reading skills by putting simple sentences about us on the blackboard, which we read out in turns. Recently I had a screaming fit over a spider crossing the room, much to the annoyance of the teacher. She wrote on the board, "Ann was frightened of a spider."

The "was frightened of a spider" was easy to read, but the first word confused me. There were hoots of laughter from the older boys when they realised that I could not read my own name.

I remember thinking then, *But it's not my name.* I was not able to voice that thought and the story stuck for a while.

For the rest of my childhood I dreaded questions about my names and who my parents were. I blushed with embarrassment when new teachers asked me to spell my surname out loud. Subsequently, I have changed my surname more than once through marriage and have not found that easy.

I should mention that from the very beginning I loved school and enjoyed learning, especially reading, writing, drawing, nature, needlework, country dancing and, best of all, singing – but not sums. I should have been able to read that sentence on the blackboard easily.

At Shirley School, I once played a trick on twin girls during playtime. They were in the outside toilets, which were always situated away from the school building and smelled of chemicals and other nasty things. I told them a frog was coming under the toilet door to get them. There was a frog nearby, and I kept them in the toilets throughout playtime with this taunt. The headmistress heard their screams and came out to collar me – literally. She picked up the frog, grabbed my collar and pretended to put the frog down my neck. I screamed harder than the girls. This was the first, but not the last, time I received the cane on my hand in front of all the school; I was about seven years old at the time.

The house where I lived was just across the road from the school, next to the church which often came in handy for me to be sent on an errand.

Once we were sent home from school because King George VI had died. I had no notion what this meant. I crossed the road and went into the cottage and said, "The king's dead."

"What are you doing here? Get back to school," replied Aunty Doris. She sent me back.

When I returned to the school, the teacher said, "Tell Mrs Shepherd you can stay at home because our king has died."

I went back home again and stated, "Our king has died." Once more, I was sent back to school.

This happened three times before a neighbour revealed the truth: there had been an announcement on the radio that King George VI had indeed died, and the whole country's schools were closed for the day as a mark of respect. I was at last allowed to go out to play.

Doris was always on the alert for 'lies', since being untruthful was a mortal sin in her eyes, and I once had soap put in my mouth for telling one. It didn't stay in long nor did it cure me. It probably made me more devious. I learned very early to withhold the truth to avoid physical punishment. I lied, as a child will, when afraid. The threat of being 'sent back' was always on her lips. Another change of home was obviously too scary for me to contemplate.

Being the one who lived nearest to the school, I was sent on an errand from school to my home from time to time. One such time, a girl had a fall at school, and the teacher asked me to run home for some butter to put on the large bump on the girl's forehead. It was a theory then that a bit of butter rubbed on a lump would reduce the swelling. I duly complied and went home.

When I arrived, Doris asked, "What are you doing here?"

"Teacher says she wants some butter," I explained.

"What for?"

"Don't know."

"Go back to school and ask her."

I scurried back.

Once I arrived back in the classroom, the teacher enquired, "Where's the butter? Hurry up, child."

"She says, what for?" I responded.

My teacher explained, and back I ran.

"It's for a lump," I told Doris when I was back home once more.

"Go back and tell her I haven't got any butter," she scolded.

It took a couple more trips back and forth till the mission was accomplished – with margarine.

The ways of grown-ups are often a mystery to a small child.

I did not know that behind-the-scenes arrangements were being put in place for my sister, who was then three, to be fostered with another couple in the village, which was presumably to try to fulfil the promise made to our mother to keep us together. I had no clear idea of our relationship when she was allowed to play with me. Apparently, we quarrelled a lot – as little children do. The couple who looked after her believed they could not have children and so were prepared to consider fostering. I understand that my sister was even more traumatised by all the moves than I had been. She did not settle well into this new arrangement. Soon, the foster mother became pregnant, and my sister, Sandra, was returned to the children's home. I was not told about this. Amazingly, as it now seems, the social worker felt that, because we two infants had squabbled, it would not be necessary to keep to the promise made to our mother to place us together.

My little sister was moved between ten different foster homes before she was finally adopted at the age of seven – hundreds of miles from me – in Northumberland. (She has found the reports describing her as "naughty and having temper tantrums" as very sad; but how could she be a well-adjusted child with so much upheaval in her young life?) I did not see Sandra again until I was twelve.

One day, when I was at home, I had misbehaved in some way – probably answering back, which was a failing I had. I was sent to my bedroom again as a punishment. I seem to have spent a lot of time in my bedroom during my young years. The room had a small cottage window, low down, with one side opening outwards.

To get released from my prison, I would often shout down, "I need a wee!" That usually resulted in a reprieve.

This strategy did not work on this particular occasion. I was told I was to stay there until bedtime. Thinking about needing a wee resulted in the inevitable: I needed more than a wee. I retrieved the chamber pot from under the bed. Using it was a hateful process for a small child – the pot was huge, and balancing with your knees bent and not spilling the contents when you stood up was very tricky. As soon as I had completed a dreaded 'number two', I realised my predicament. I had been warned severely that a 'number two' was for the outside toilet only. I opened the window and looked down. Beneath me was a path running along the edge of a small lawn. A dustbin stood on the path by a wall. No one appeared, so I fetched the pot and tipped the contents out of the window. Luckily, it landed behind the bin. I never confessed. The binmen came, and I expected the worst. The matter was never mentioned again. I like to think of Doris's embarrassment when the binmen came and moved the bin. She could hardly blame the dog.

❦

From a report by The Children's Society's welfare officer in August 1952, when I was six, I learned that my mother had written to my foster mother. She hoped that she could visit me. My mother never came.

By the time I was eight, a report mentions my foster mother saying that I had been very troublesome lately, both cheeky and disobedient; the phrase "very talkative" began to appear in many of these reports. Aged nine I was still "deliberately disobedient" according to Doris, but I had promised the social worker I would try harder to be good.

This reminds me of a funny story about my grandson, Dylan, with whom my husband John and I share a very close relationship. One New Year's Day, when Dylan was seven, he and I were alone having an early breakfast at his home. I asked him if he knew what day it was, and he replied, "January 1st."

I told him that people often made promises called resolutions on New Year's Day and I wanted him to make one with me.

Quick as a flash he said, "Well, what are you going to promise, Grandma?"

"I'm going to try to give up drinking red wine and eating chocolates, because I need to lose some weight," I replied.

"And what do I have to do?"

"I would like you to try not to be cheeky to your mum and dad. You know they love you very much, but it is very difficult for them when you answer back all the time."

"I don't!"

"There you go. You can think things, but keep quiet sometimes."

He promised to try.

The next day, as we left them, he looked at my husband and then at me, and said, "Keep an eye on her for me, will you, John?"

The same time the next year we forgot to renew our resolutions and Dylan reminded me, "We haven't done those promise things, Grandma."

"Well," I said. "How do you think you did last year?"

"Not bad, but you didn't do very well either, did you? I've seen you drinking red wine!"

CHAPTER THREE
Cottage Discomforts

THE SMALL BRICK COTTAGE IN SHIRLEY VILLAGE WAS attached to its neighbour, and had a tunnel between the houses that ran under a bedroom. This space was whitewashed once a year by our next-door neighbour, Harry, who lived in the attached house with his wife Bessie and their two sons. They were a friendly, happy family, and I remember Harry teasing me at Christmas about Santa Claus, by asking me if I had heard those noisy reindeer. At age six, I declared that I was going to marry their youngest son, Ian. Incidentally, many years later, he married J, a blind teacher of music, and she and I became good friends, and we shared many interesting experiences together – but that's another story.

Our cottage had two rooms downstairs with a staircase closed off by a door, to stop the heat escaping upwards. Upstairs in the cottage there were two bedrooms. A door off the kitchen opened onto the staircase leading directly onto the floor of the first bedroom, thus presenting a dark hole, which I was afraid of falling down when I was small.

The bedrooms were never heated – it would have been thought unhealthy – and there was no central heating, although some houses had a fireplace in the bedrooms. Throughout all my childhood, for much of the year I woke up in a cold room and struggled to put my clothes on under the blankets, which was torture, especially in winter. There were no duvets, just cold sheets and itchy, grey blankets tucked in tightly on all sides. The room downstairs had a large stone sink, a black-lead grate and a red-tiled floor that had to be scrubbed every week with Cardinal Red polish applied, which was messy and very staining. Household tasks were dirty, hard work and completed without any electrical appliances, such as a vacuum cleaner, electric kettle or fridge. Water was heated in a brick-lined boiler, which would have been fired underneath in former times. The fireplace had an oven and a compartment for boiling water. The grate had to have black-lead polish applied once a week and then buffed for ages to make it shine – small cracks were cleaned with an old toothbrush – and the ashes were scattered on the garden each morning to improve the soil. I loathed both these jobs that were part of my Saturday morning chores as I became older and took up a lot of playing time, especially as there was always a row before I was forced to get down to it. Likewise, I had to clean all the many objects made of brass that decorated the cottage's oak beams, as was the fashion then. There were brass candleholders, a coal scuttle, horseshoes, a copper kettle, a teapot stand, a toasting fork and a curious thing called a 'companion set', which was a stand holding items to keep the hearth clean and tidy – this was a nightmare to clean with Brasso polish, rags and an old toothbrush.

Coal was delivered once a fortnight on a lorry – by the hundredweight in dirty, black sacks – to each house in the village, and it was stored in an outhouse at the top of the garden, next to the dreaded toilet. The 'coal men' were always covered in black grime, and I wondered if that was their real colour. I can still recall the sound of coal being shovelled into a coal scuttle and brought into the house. We supplemented the coal supply with firewood gathered on daily walks in the woods with Doris and her two dogs, which were treated with the affection and kisses that I never received. We would return down Park Lane, laden with bags of logs and my little basket full of twigs to be dried in the range oven.

Using the outdoor toilet at the end of the long garden path was a great trial for me. It was housed in a small brick building with a wooden door, which had holes in and a latch too high for me to reach. It was freezing in winter. The only light in the toilet when the door was closed came from the cracks in and under the door. The walls were whitewashed, and strung with cobwebs and huge spiders. I was very afraid that the spiders would bite me. The toilet was a large bucket that was placed underneath a wooden shelf in which there was a big hole. I often visited another cottage where the seat had two spaces side by side. The hole looked huge and frightening to me and the smell was not good either. A liquid called Jeyes Fluid, which was in a large metal can, was splashed down the hole from time to time to mask the smell and add some disinfecting properties. Looking down I could discern a dark, evil floating mess. The toilet paper was made from sheets of newspaper cut into squares, which were hung on a length of string fastened onto a nail hammered into the wall.

This building was the source of great terror to me and made going to the toilet difficult to say the least. To compensate, I was dosed with a spoonful of syrup of figs each morning, which I loved the taste of, and a spoonful of cod liver oil, which I hated. It is difficult to believe now that the contents of the toilet were disposed of into a hole dug in the garden, winter and summer. There were no mains sewers or septic tanks in that area in those days. The soil in this part of the garden would be crawling with evil-looking worms and could not be used for growing things. Neighbours would chat away across the gardens whilst carrying out this weekly chore on their own patch. Tom used to loathe this job, and would tie a handkerchief over his nose and mouth to reduce the smell. I thought he was being a cowboy, like on the television.

—∞∞∞—

Bath time and hair washing was a once-a-week ritual. A large, coffin-shaped tin bath was shared between households (on different nights of the week). It was placed in front of the fire, and the water had to be heated bit by bit in a pan on the fire. I was bathed first, with carbolic soap, which was hard and smelly – there were no shampoos or conditioners in the average working-class house in the 1950s. The adults would follow, sharing the water, and I don't know what else when I was safely in bed and out of the way. How different it is from today's daily showers and hair products.

Our hair must have been very greasy by the end of the week, as our brushes and combs were often full of grease. Most local women wore a headscarf tied with a knot at the front, often with rows of hair rollers underneath; an overall to protect their clothes whilst doing their housework, as houses were fairly dirty places with coal fires; and always a hat when they went out. Having to wash my very straight hair several times a week nowadays, I can understand why hats were worn so much. The luxury of a bathroom with a fitted bath, hot water in the taps and showers was many years away for the average household.

I had moved from the poverty of a poor London street to a rural village deep in the countryside in a few short years. Yet I have always felt that this was the best thing that happened to me, in spite of all I had lost and all the unhappiness in my foster home. I learned to love country life; I grew to know every kind of wild flower, birdsong, tree and wild animal. Nature study was my favourite subject for a while, because the teacher would take us out in the fields to identify flowers, trees, etc. We had a nature table in the classroom to display the things we found, and wild flowers were labelled and stuck in jam jars full of water. Being the 'class monitor' who kept the table tidy and threw away dead flowers with their stinky water, was one of my proudest jobs.

We children could roam in the woods and fields freely out of school time, only knowing we needed to go home when the local men working around the estate said, "It's teatime; you'd best be off home or you'll catch it!"

I have loved being outdoors all my life despite my origins in the great city. I have shared this love with my children and now my grandchildren, who have the same enjoyment.

My grandson Dylan once remarked, "Sometimes it's just like being at school with Grandma because she's always saying things like, 'Look at that flower', or 'Just listen to that birdsong.'" He developed an interest in birds for a while, so all was not wasted.

Both my sons have grown up with a love of the countryside and outdoor activities.

CHAPTER FIVE

What's the Gossip?

THE VILLAGE AND MOST OF ITS PROPERTIES BELONGED AT
that time to the estate of a local landowner. The village farms supplied
produce for the manor house. Many of the local men worked on the
farms or as woodsmen in the extensive wooded land that stretched
between the two estate villages belonging to the same family. All the
villagers knew each other and their business. There were fewer than
a hundred cottages and farms built around the main lane in Shirley
village at that time.

Next to the school there was a post office and small shop, an ancient
pub, the church and several farms opening onto the main street. The
sound of cows walking up the lane from the fields for milking time,
the hum of the milking machines, the clank of the heavy churns being
rolled across to the milk stand for collection by the milk lorry – these
were the daily background noise to village life. Traffic was almost
unknown. We children played in the main street all day, and a passing
tractor, horses or the occasional delivery van could easily be heard
and avoided.

Shopping for food was very different. There was rationing, of
course, for a few years, and I remember the delivery vans that would
arrive in the middle of the village, whose drivers would open the
doors at the back and display their wares. On different days of the

week, there would be a butcher, a grocer, a greengrocer, a baker and a fishmonger. To summon customers, some rang a noisy handbell, whilst others tooted their horn. They had an art in arranging all the goods to tempt the housewives, with some special offers, even in those days.

'Mr Kleeneze', a travelling salesman, walked through the villages occasionally with his suitcase of items to demonstrate many new products – brushes, cloths, cleaning fluids and pastes, and other essential wares for the modern housewife. There was always a gathering of women who would catch up on the gossip and all the tittle-tattle tales of the village. As I grew older I used to try to listen in to all their complaining, from behind the entry door. I tried to figure out the meaning of such pronouncements as these: "She'll get her comeuppance one of these days you mark my words!"; "Well, of course, he's three sheets to the wind and his mother went doolally before she was done, so what can you expect?"; "You can't put old heads on young shoulders, that's what I say. She'll laugh on the other side of her face before she's done."; and "You'd best watch your tongue; walls have ears!"

More than once, I heard myself discussed in exasperated terms by my irate foster mother. I must have been very difficult to manage.

———◦◦◦———

When I was a small child, I could not go out to play in cold weather until I was dressed up in wellingtons; long, grey socks; a beret; a coat with a belt, a scarf tightly knotted around my neck; and mittens on a piece of elastic threaded through my sleeves, so I didn't lose them. A spare hanky was a must – it was tucked into the small, purpose-made pocket of my navy-blue knickers. Imagine having to hitch your clothes up to find a handkerchief to blow your nose.

Once, my then three-year-old grandson William, when asked by me if he wanted a hanky as he swept his arm across his nose, looked at me with a puzzled expression and said, "What's a hanky, Grandma?"

Underneath all this outdoor clobber I had to wear a vest; a liberty bodice for warmth, which had rubber buttons attached (whatever were they for?); a grey tunic dress; a long-sleeved blouse; and a hand-knitted, grey, woollen cardigan. I could hardly move with all that on and often 'lost' some items along the way.

When we were out playing with other children, we enjoyed all the traditional games. 'Sheep, sheep, come home' was one of my favourites and so was 'The Farmer's in His Den' – in which I always got picked for the dog and was 'patted' mercilessly. We learned to skip and bat a ball against a wall. I played inside the trunk of the old, gnarled, broken tree against the church wall opposite our cottage, with my tea set and my dolls. The ancient tree and its hollowed-out insides still stands, and it shoots a halo of green foliage in spring. We could play in the lane all day with little interruption from the occasional tractor, horse or car going past.

How different from that is the same village street now, with many parked vehicles, new houses and constant traffic flowing through. The schoolroom is a smart bungalow and the headteacher's house is a much-improved country cottage. There were no new houses in and around the village in the 1950s; it was much as it had been for many generations: a small, peaceful hamlet in rural countryside, accessed from two winding country lanes a mile from the main road.

CHAPTER SIX

The Rhythms of Life

THROUGH THE SEASONS, LIFE IN THE VILLAGE HAD ITS rhythms and rituals that we children grew to love. We could search for snowdrops and violets in the hedgerows in spring. I could name all the hedgerow flowers that were growing in abundance – pink campion, lady's smock, meadowsweet, foxgloves, egg and bacon, speedwell, love lies bleeding and many more. We paddled in streams, carrying a jam jar on a string to collect frog spawn, which would stand on a window ledge in the school until the tadpoles developed into little frogs – or died in the slimy water. Bright, shiny conkers were gathered eagerly as soon as they dropped; conker fights were the thing. Boys would collect handfuls and take them home to harden them off in the oven overnight. Girls were not so keen; the boys always tried to hit our knuckles or get us out because they said we were cissy when we cried, nursing our stinging fingers. We girls would rather play skipping, hopscotch or other group games.

For us children, there would be the excitement of picking blackberries down the lanes in late August, returning home with hands and mouths stained bright red, and tingling from the prickly thorns. We searched for wild mushrooms in September in fields where cows had roamed – always hoping they hadn't trodden on the best ones first. Families gathered holly with bright red berries just before

Christmas, reaching the best branches with a borrowed walking stick and shrieking at the prickles as bunches fell to the ground. We sought out fir cones and mistletoe from an old apple tree in winter, to decorate the house and the church, and breathed in the smell of pine needles. Year by year, we experienced mounting excitement as the great day approached.

The harvest provided us with fun in fields of new-mown hay, which we could throw and roll about in. There were no baling machines in those days to process the hay, which would lie in the fields to dry off and await the arrival of the gang of men who shared the task of getting in the hay for all the local farms. It was hard and dangerous work for them – they stood on top of the loaded cart as it swayed on its way up or down lanes to the farmyard haystack or hayrick. Gone are the rolling, grassy fields where, with arms aloft, we would tumble over and over – ground to sky and sky to grass – gathering purple clover in our hair. Now, down country lanes at dusk, the roar of the farm equipment followed by trailers laden with plastic-covered bales announces the end of harvest, all done by one man and a machine.

There were no refrigerators or freezers, so everything that grew and could be processed to last through the winter months was collected. At home, we children would be coerced to help with 'topping and tailing' gooseberries; picking damsons off the laden fruit trees; collecting apples and home-grown tomatoes, and peeling them to make jams and chutneys; and eating as many fruits as we could stuff our faces with before we were spotted. Kilner jars – stout glass bottles with a rubber seal and metal sealing clasp – were brought out and prepared for holding the sliced pears, damsons and plums, over which would be poured boiling water from the whistling kettle on the range – making sure that there were no air bubbles to turn the fruit mouldy. I remember collecting elderflowers and their berries to make fragrant drinks, and going round the cottages to beg for empty bottles to take to the shop or pub to get a penny or two refunded. It was all hard work, but we learned many homemaking skills as girls, which certainly helped me when I came to run my own home.

Autumn – with the smell and crunch of fallen leaves, the riotous colours and the rituals of this close-knit countryside – has always fascinated me. Soon would follow the church's harvest service. Local women and men would spend a lot of evenings decorating the church with produce – vegetables and fruits, much of it grown in the village. Women would have been hard at work making pickles, and bottling and jamming the fruit to last the winter. A local baker would provide the traditional bread sheaf. At the harvest service, the church had a special smell of vegetables, bread and sheaves of wheat, and the hymns to celebrate and give thanks were always the same: 'We Plough the Fields and Scatter', 'Come, Ye Thankful People, Come' and 'All Is Safely Gathered In'. Wartime rationing meant that what was grown on the land was a welcome addition to a limited diet and tight budget. All fresh foods had their season; there were never strawberries at Christmas.

Next came the harvest supper, which is a tradition that still survives in our town and in many local rural villages. This was a jolly occasion, which took place in the schoolroom, for villagers to share a meal from some of the produce, and it was sometimes followed by an auction of leftovers and a glass or two of home-made wine. Regular entertainment was provided with whist drives for the grown-ups and 'beetle drives' for children, which is a simple drawing game where players move around tables to a different partner after each game. The usual children's chatter was frowned upon.

There were visits to the homes of friends and neighbours at Christmas, and a 'party tea' of sandwiches, pork pie, tinned peaches with bread and butter, and, if you were lucky, fairy cakes with marzipan fruit on top would be provided. The decorated Christmas cake took pride of place, which had been baked some weeks before; it was rich and dark, with lots of fruit and a pint of ale, and laced with a drop of brandy each week to keep it moist. Housewives would have to save coupons every week throughout the year toward the dividend (divi) at the Co-operative (Co-op) shop where these special luxuries could be bought. Christmas puddings, which were mixed and stirred and steamed for hours, were a feature of many housewives' duties. Some added a silver sixpence in the mix – to be found by hungry children and claimed as their prize.

On these special gatherings of neighbours and friends, I would be put to bed in a strange, cold bed, whilst the grown-ups played whist downstairs after supper, and then I'd be lifted and carried home half-asleep at the end of the party, down the icy lane back to my own cold bed. I can recall vividly the strangeness of these occasions. Once, at a gathering, a special photographer came to take photos of the children. I was whisked back home and arranged, with my hair combed and my best winter frock on, to have my photo taken. I discovered many decades later that this picture was to be sent to my mother, who had been asking The Children's Society for a photograph of me.

With the excitement of Christmas, school time would be given over to making paper streamers from long pieces of coloured paper, each of which was formed into a circle and glued at the ends, with one passed through another to link them together. There was a concert to be performed in front of parents, the rehearsals for which were taken very seriously, and it was agony waiting to be chosen to sing. I loved to sing and could easily memorise all the words to songs.

Carol singing around the village and school parties would follow. At home, a small 'real' Christmas tree would appear; there were no artificial trees around. 'Dressing the tree' was a Christmas Eve ceremony in our house. The decorations were made of glass and very fragile; there was no tinsel or Santa toys. The house would be decorated with holly and ivy, which would be arranged around a mirror or picture, but not until the last few days leading up to 25th December. The notion of starting Christmas in the autumn was thankfully not around. Christmas cards were only sent to those family members who lived away from the village, and certainly not to each other.

I remember the feeling of excitement when the first snowflakes fell, and waking up on a cold winter's morning to find everything covered in white, with the footsteps of a chirpy robin and next-door's cat the only marks on the garden. The fun of building a snowman, sledging down the fields and gathering dry sticks in the woods for the fire are vivid images in my mind. Frozen patterns made by the frost on window panes were a fascination of mine. At school we were taught how to fold paper and snip out bits to make a paper snowflake. If you snipped the wrong corner, it all fell apart.

I can recall being sent on errands around the village, when I was about six or seven, such as to a farm along the lane for eggs, for which I had a little wicker basket.

If I arrived at the farmhouse's back door as the local men got back from the fields for their breakfast, they would tease me mercilessly. "Hello, what do you want?" they would say, smiling but pretending not to know me. They would put a china egg in my basket alongside five speckled eggs and ask me to count them. They would pretend to fetch eggs, but bring back a bunch of rhubarb from the kitchen garden, wrapped up neatly in a large leaf. Once, they put a live chick in my basket instead of eggs. I cried when I could not keep it. They were a kind, hard-working group of men, and I am sure they enjoyed teasing any of the local children they came across.

I was sometimes sent to the dairy of another farm down the hill, with a jug and money to fetch cream on special days. I was also sent to the back door of the pub on Sundays, with another jug for a pint of ale. Everyone got to know me; I gather I was a chatty child and always had a lot to say. I must have been quite an oddity in the village, since fostering was not common and my cockney accent made me different from the other village children.

Like in all small villages, there were memorable characters. The church sexton who rang the bells twice every Sunday seemed very old to me at the time, and I was fascinated to learn that he rang the three bells on his own, with a rope in each hand and one with his foot. The space up in the loft where he rang the bells – after climbing steep, narrow stairs – is tiny; he had to balance on one leg. I don't remember any unintended clangers. His wife was very stern and a scold; children were wary of a ball landing in her garden – it was seldom returned, and we would get a telling-off for letting it stray.

—⊸∞⊶—

At the bottom of the main street was the village shop and post office, run by Mr and Mrs J. When I was old enough to go there, I would dress up my doll, put her carefully in the grey pram, with its hood down in fine weather, and off I trundled. All the village folk spoke to me, admiring my dolly whom I called Susan. There was hardly any traffic and I was quite safe.

Next to the shop was the red telephone box with its black box and shiny silver buttons: A and B for connections, and C to get your money back. The telephone number was Brailsford 248 as I recall; there was no code, it was connected by a real person, and for a while I believed the operator was inside the shop. When I was older, I would arrange to talk to my boyfriend secretly at the red telephone box and would wait anxiously outside for it to ring, whilst trying to hide from villagers who might report me to my foster mother. That telephone box is still intact, but without its black phone, and has now been turned into a village lending library.

On the opposite corner was the milk stand. Herds of cows, heavy with milk, would wander down the village street twice a day. At each farm, after milking, the milk underwent a cleansing and cooling process through a machine – rather like a washboard – and then it was stored in churns. We would hear the sound of the milk churns being rolled down the street to the milk stand, from where the milk lorry collected them to take to the dairy to put into glass bottles. Cream would be extracted from some of the milk to sell to villagers or to supplement the feed of new calves. Everybody drank only full-cream milk in those days.

The milk stand became the place where children would gather in the school holidays and on Saturdays, to decide which games to play. There would be about half a dozen of us of mixed ages, and the older boys would often decide to go off into Shirley woods. The woodlands and the villages of Shirley and Osmaston were part of the estate of Osmaston Manor, which were owned by the Walker-Okeover family at that time. Many of the men of the villages worked as woodsmen, blacksmiths or gamekeepers on the estate, and they would look out for the children of both villages as they wandered in the woods. There was never any fear of us children being unsafe.

Now the village school has morphed into two smart country cottages, with neat gardens, hedges, lawns and rose beds where the school field and playground once was our little world. The village pub has a smart restaurant where the tap room used to be, serves gourmet meals to visitors and the many ramblers who pass through. The little shop and post office are long gone. The milk stand is mere rotting boards amongst the weeds and vehicles parked outside the pub.

One unusual building that still exists deep within the woods is the sawmill, which was built in grey stone in the design of a Swiss cottage, with low eaves and a mock bell tower, complete with bell. This was the place where the timber felled in the woods was brought by carts to be processed for hedge and gate posts. A small rail track ran along the front of the building. This transported the bogeys carrying the timber to the benches where it was cut into squared posts by a circular saw.

At the side of the sawmill, water from the nearby lake ran through a horizontal trough and over the large waterwheel, which collected then disgorged the water back into the wheel race beneath. Inside the building, the turning of the wheel drove the belt that worked the saw that cut the timber. Behind the wheel stood a mysterious structure resembling a large wishing well. It was filled with creosote and smelled very evil. The timber that had been cut and planed inside the sawmill was hoisted onto a small track that ran to the edge of the creosote pit. The fence posts and farm gates were hauled by chains and dipped into the foul liquid. Finally, they were neatly piled on the footpath, ready to be transported around the estate to repair fences and gates. Some would be sold to the local farms, and were collected by each farmer on a tractor. The wood pile seethed with rats. It was a scary place, but the smells and sounds of all this industry were fascinating to children, though they were forbidden to go there.

The sawmill was a wonderful old building. I have, over many years, walked there with my own children, grandchildren and many friends. Such is our affection for this place that, in my husband's and my apartment, we have a beautiful oil painting of the sawmill in winter, painted by my son David, and a further watercolour of the same building in summer, painted by a local artist. The sawmill has been silent for decades now, but – thanks to recent English Heritage funding – it has been restored to some of its former glory, though sadly not as a working mill.

The blacksmith's forge stands nearby, idle and overgrown. When I was a child, it was a busy place, with the blacksmith shoeing the horses working on the estate and for hunters' horses. One reminder of the blacksmith's skill is a double seat made entirely from horseshoes, which stands at the edge of the nearby village pond. We regularly saw riders in the village. Horses were exercised in the woods regularly, and the hunt would meet outside the village pub, The Saracen's Head, on Boxing Day for their tipple before riding off into the woods. We were prohibited from playing there at hunting time and during the shooting season. Men were employed to rear pheasants in the wood in readiness for the 'guns'. Pheasants were sometimes sold to villagers at Christmastime. How sad it was to see their lifeless, hanging heads and colourful feathers.

Foxes were a problem to the farmers and estate staff at this time because of the many pheasants being fattened for Christmas fare. I remember seeing a nest of baby foxes once and being worried in case a farmer should find and shoot them.

Rabbits were everywhere and were shot enthusiastically and given to the villagers for cooking. I can recall Tom grimacing at trying to skin a rabbit with Doris scolding him for the mangled result. Similarly, plucking a chicken or pheasant always produced much domestic stress, and I hated the black tubes in the cooked chicken from where the feathers had been pulled out too roughly. After we began to see rabbits poisoned with myxomatosis during the cull in the 1950s, we stopped eating them. It was distressing to me to see a stumbling, blind and drooling baby rabbit on the footpaths; it gave me nightmares afterwards. I have never knowingly eaten rabbit since.

The estate has a number of man-made lakes and natural streams, which attracted us to paddle, search for pond life and mess about generally. There were numerous things to look out for: mushrooms in autumn, bluebells in spring, rabbits and their babies, hares, pheasants, swans and birds' nests, which all the children were warned not to plunder. I was threatened severely with dire consequences if I strayed near the lakeside, and one particular stagnant pond at the side of the lane was especially forbidden. One day, whilst playing with the twin girls who lived on an estate farm, we strayed into the nearby fields looking for birds' nests in the hedgerows. Whilst climbing a gate, I slipped and landed in a large puddle. It was Monday, which was washday.

There were no electric washing machines around at that time. Washing clothes was done by hand and took ages. The boiler had to be heated; a metal dolly tub was dragged out of the garden shed; hot water was ladled in by hand; a dolly peg made of copper, which was shaped like a child's spinning top with holes in, was used to swish the clothes around in the hot water; and the wet clothes were fed from the tub using wooden tongs into a hand-turned mangle, then returned to the tub for rinsing. All the water was carried by hand, and the whole process was carried out on the back yard, whatever the weather.

Clothes were dried outdoors on a washing line in fine weather and indoors, draped over a wooden clothes horse, when it was wet. One of my memories of my childhood is the smell of laundry drying around the cottage.

Some cotton items had to be rinsed in starch, which is a powder that is dissolved in water and makes cotton items go stiff when dry. Sometimes a 'blue bag' was used to make white clothes brighter.

Ironing was a long, arduous process, particularly when cotton garments had been starched. Irons had no steam facility, so if cotton clothes were too dry to iron water would be sprinkled across the item, which was then rolled into a sausage shape to avoid more wrinkles, making the item fit to proceed with. There was a particular way to iron every item; shirts had to be ironed in order of collars, cuffs, sleeves, fronts and then the back, and folded just so. Washday was a long, stressful and exhausting process, which was typical of many of the household tasks that all women had to do and that seem to take no time at all these days with modern machinery. It's small wonder most women could not find time to go out to work.

So, I knew I would be in trouble on that day when I fell in the puddle for going home wet through and muddy at the end of the weekly wash. Apparently, according to our neighbours' gossip, my crying could be heard long before I reached home and the expected scolding duly followed.

"How many times have I told you to keep away from that pond?" my foster mother demanded to know. "You are such a naughty girl."

"But I didn't go in the pond," I sobbed.

"Just look at the state of you. I've just finished the washing as well. You are a very naughty little girl. What have I told you about that pond? I've told you time and time again not to tell lies. If you keep on telling lies, we will send you away, and you will have to go to a home for naughty girls."

I had no idea where such a place could be.

I recall being most upset because I couldn't explain that I had fallen off a gate into a puddle. This seemed to me to be most unfair. I became very fearful of the 'home for naughty girls' too. Only recently did I understand from a television programme how great was the risk of contracting polio in the 1950s from bathing in unclean water, so adults were understandably cautious about children straying into ponds and lakes.

I spent a lot of my growing-up years thinking life was very unfair. The 'deceit' I began to perfect was to avoid the nagging and the beating. When smacked, I learned to stop screaming so that she would stop hitting me; she was also mindful of the neighbours hearing. I think my feelings were more pained than my hand or leg that received the smack. My lonely thoughts turned to hatred for the unloving face that only saw in me a burdensome, irritating child. I knew nothing about 'love', but I certainly felt that lack of closeness. A hug, an encouraging smile or a kiss, which I observed in other children's houses, were what I missed.

Unbeknownst to me, our neighbours were quizzed by The Children's Society's social worker about my care, from time to time. I never knew that anyone was interested in my welfare or happiness; her visits would usually be an opportunity for my foster mother to complain about my behaviour, and for me to be berated by my foster mother for my many misdemeanours. Years later, I was able to read the social-work reports about these visits to the house. It is clear that my foster mother's harsh regime was discussed frequently within The Children's Society. The decisions to leave things as they were must have been based on my obvious enjoyment of school and my progress there. Resentment grew inside my young head, and, eventually, it led to rebellion.

When I couldn't go out to play in bad weather, I led a fairly solitary existence at home. Children were never invited into our house. I began to fill my time with reading. I would pester Tom each Wednesday for a copy of *School Friend*, my favourite comic. I read any book I could get hold of and this helped me a lot with school work. Maths held terrors for me in spite of learning tables by rote at primary school, with whole-class chanting; I never really got the hang of numbers, and maths lessons at secondary school were a constant worry. I was, however, good at reading, writing and languages, and I loved the lessons when these subjects were taught. I liked sports, but was not particularly energetic or skilled at any.

Doris managed to get help to teach me some maths prior to the dreaded eleven-plus, and I passed. I was the only child in the village to pass the exam that year. This fact isolated me from the other village children, who then went to the secondary modern school. There was a great deal of snobbery about attending the grammar school in those days, which was before comprehensive schools were created.

Despite going to the 'better' school, my abilities in maths after this did not improve significantly. We had one particular maths teacher who would pick on the weakest, which included me, and require us to go to the blackboard at the front of the class and work out a problem in public. How that was ever going to build knowledge and confidence, I have no idea. I felt sick and very unhappy before every maths lesson. I never felt able to admit that I could not understand. When taking my general certificate of education (GCE), I completed my name on the exam papers and little else.

Tom's one passion in life was football. He would follow the Derby County team every week. He never went to away games, but supported the team at every home game – nothing could get in the way of this. Often, he would take other men from the village to the match, because he had a car, and there were not many car owners in the village. Every Saturday, he would get going earlier in the day than usual, much to the irritation of Doris, to get his paper round finished in time to get to the match.

On one memorable Saturday, she was particularly upset with him and decided to lock the doors whilst he was getting changed to stop him going out. I cowered in the kitchen fearing a row involving me.

Tom rushed about, eating his sandwiches on the run. After preparing to leave, he went to the back door. He looked about him with a puzzled expression and said, "What have you done with the key?"

The outcome, after a few more hot words, was that Tom opened a window overlooking the lane and jumped out, to cheers from the waiting men; they all got in the car and off they sped to the football match. Doris was raging and I hid from her anger.

This period seemed to mark a serious deterioration in the household, and the silence was acute. I often heard Doris, when she was angry, standing at the door of our long-suffering neighbour bewailing Tom's deficiencies as she saw them. Our neighbour was a kind, friendly soul who realised how things really stood and would try to soften her anger, but to no avail. It was a very difficult time for all of us. Tom would spend as much time as possible out of the house. He was reported to spend time doing his book work in his car inside the garage he rented along the lane.

I was young and knew nothing of the nature of married life, but my foster parents' deteriorating relationship gave me no insights for my later years – other than the power of silence.

CHAPTER SEVEN

The Dark Side of Care

THERE WAS ONE DARK EVENT IN MY CHILDHOOD THAT HAD lasting effects on me. I can't remember why, but one afternoon, when I was about seven, I was given a lift home from Ashbourne to Shirley in the car of a male friend of my foster parents, who had undertaken to help me with my sums before the eleven-plus exam. I was sitting in the front passenger seat (there were no seatbelts in those days), chattering away, as usual.

I can still picture the man's leering smile as he reached across suddenly with his left arm and said, "You're a nice little girl, aren't you?" He slid his hand up my leg and pushed his fingers into my knickers.

I was so shocked and frightened that I grabbed the door handle immediately. The car was slowing down to turn right, and I fell out onto the road – grazing my arm, face and legs, and was dragged along the road, away from the car. The man got out of the car and came over to me, and I screamed and cried hysterically as he put me back in the car and drove me home. I don't remember him saying anything until we arrived back. He told Doris that I had opened the door and fallen out. She of course reacted by shouting at me for being naughty.

I expect I was sent to bed after some first aid. I certainly was not cuddled. I could not explain what had really happened. I did not understand what had occurred; it was a horrible experience, and it made me very scared and wary of men. I began having nightmares, imagining that my bedroom was expanding on all sides and that I became tiny with the room swallowing me up. This continued for a few years, but I never spoke about them. These nightmares may be a common experience for abused children – I have heard others speak of the same feelings – but they made me very fearful of the dark, and I begged to keep the light on at night. I began to have what I now believe were panic attacks, and would sometimes faint. Strangely, I got some warm attention for a while from Doris when this happened, who seemed worried by my sudden attacks. I don't know if these events were reported to the social worker, but the 'family friend' was never seen again at the house.

In recent years, we have become all too familiar with the behaviour of paedophiles. Happily, children are now more likely to be heard and believed. The long-term effects on adults too are much more widely understood. Unfortunately, this was not the only time I was abused by a man.

<hr />

I became aware as I grew older that some people regard abandoned children as responsible for their own past and therefore as less worthy. Any naughty behaviour was seen as being a result of bad genes. It is difficult for some people to hear about deprivation and to believe the effects it can have long term. I always wanted to be just like other children. I was embarrassed by my lack of family, my strange names and my past history, and I learned very early in my life to bury bad memories and to avoid questions about my family. I always knew I was different in some way, but not why or how. I was about thirteen when it finally dawned on me that I was alone in the world, with no one to really love and care about me. It made me very determined to show them how clever I could be, especially Doris, who was the enemy in my head by this time. I never asked to be taken away from her because I had only a vague awareness of what that might mean, but it did not sound good.

In spite of my unhappiness at home, I have often reflected that if my early life had followed its natural course, I would never have had all these experiences of nature and village life, and all the opportunities and freedom to enjoy them. Life in London would have been so much different.

———

When I was nine, Shirley village school closed because of small numbers and the retirement of the headmistress. I was sent to the school at Brailsford, a village with a larger population, straddling the main A52 road. It was about two miles away, and I had to rely on Tom to take me there every morning as he started his paper round. Tom was self-employed, delivering newspapers and magazines to many farms and outlying local villages that had no shop. He had built the business up when he returned from war service, and was widely known and liked in the farming communities. It must have been hard for him to earn a decent living; he travelled over a wide area and his round took all day. He would also set out early in the evening to deliver the *Derby Evening Telegraph* to some of the same farms and villages.

At the beginning of his day, Tom would pick up the parcels of newspapers and magazines that the wholesaler had delivered at the end of the lane, next to the main road. He had made a stout wooden box with a lid, which was left by the roadside, and the parcels of newspapers were put in it. Sometimes, if there was a different delivery man, the parcels were thrown into the hedgerow, and in wet weather Tom would have to take the parcels home and dry out the wet newspapers. He was never up and about early enough to meet the delivery van. I can remember vividly the smell of wet pages of newsprint hanging around the kitchen drying off around the Aga, before he could recommence his round.

He had a Morris Minor estate, and he used to arrange the

newspapers and magazines in piles in the back of the car in the order that he had to deliver them. He was skilled at grabbing a newspaper from behind him whilst steering the car and smoking a cigarette as he sped down winding country lanes. He would jump out, barely stopping the car, leaving the engine running whilst he ran from house to house or farm gate. He put the papers in a convenient drainpipe or box to be collected by the farm hands or housewives.

Everybody for many miles around knew him and loved him. He was always friendly and very polite, but let it be known that he never had time to stop and chat, as he ran back to his vehicle and off to the next place.

His customers never complained if he was late delivering their daily paper. They would smile and remark, "Oh well. That's Tom for you!"

This was the age when few people had a car, so Tom's deliveries were appreciated. It was also before the great petrol crisis in the early 1970s, when the steep rise in the cost of fuel made it difficult for him to make a decent income.

Tom had grown up in rural Shropshire on the family farm. His war service was his first and only experience of life away from the countryside. He was always reluctant to speak about that time. Tom did everything at a slow and measured pace, apart from when he was delivering newspapers. One day in the early 1960s, one of his customers saw him looking very ill with a dreadful cough. The man tried to persuade him to see a doctor. Tom said he had no time for doctors. Eventually, he collapsed on his paper round and had to be taken to hospital. He was very sick for some while. He was in the cottage hospital in Ashbourne for a few weeks, with pneumonia, and he never recovered his original energy again – he continued to smoke a lot. He always had a hacking cough, but believed that a fag would cure it. There was an immediate need for someone to take on his job. His brother-in-law tried to do this and had to call in extra help. The two men said they were amazed at how much work Tom accomplished every day, alone.

In 1954, when I had to change school, Tom was responsible for getting me there because it was too far for me to walk to Brailsford village alone at the age of nine. The school was the first stop on his route after picking up and sorting his newspapers. We were always late for the start of school. I suffered agonies because I had to walk into a room where everyone was in the middle of assembly, and it led to a lifelong anxiety about being late for appointments. The headteacher, to his credit marked my attendance records on my reports as "never late". He obviously knew the score.

The first day the teacher asked me to say my full names, the other children giggled. Thereafter, my nickname was 'Vee-nees' or 'Heinz Baked Beans rhymes with Venes'. Children can be cruel but imaginative too. I always wished that I had a name that people could spell easily, so I wouldn't have to face those agonies.

I enjoyed being at that school too. There was an emphasis on music, dancing and drama, which I loved. Usually, I anxiously wanted to be a star, but was mostly unable to push myself forward. I got over it. An elderly teacher, the widow of a previous headmaster, played the piano, and led us in country dancing and singing every week. We learned many folk songs and the school choir was entered in a choir competition, which was a novel experience for country children. I remember learning songs such as 'They're Changing Guards at Buckingham Palace', 'The Ash Grove', 'How Much Is That Doggy in the Window' and 'I Saw Mummy Kissing Santa Claus', and I developed the ability to memorise the words to all the tunes. I was once persuaded to sing on stage at a children's outdoor concert in Llandudno, and I got a prize for singing 'My Bonnie Lies Over the Ocean'. This was the start of my amateur 'singing career'.

The tradition of folk dancing was also taught, and we had some fun learning barn dances, maypole dancing, square dancing and the Gay Gordons. A television company came to the school once and filmed the activities of a traditional village school, including our country dancing. I appeared briefly. Many decades later, my nephew saw the film during a documentary on television about bygone village life, and I managed to obtain a copy. It was strange to see myself on film as a nine-year-old.

At Christmastime, the whole school was involved in a concert for parents and villagers. This caused great excitement, and there were lots of rehearsals. One year, the staff and headteacher did a little play at the end of our concert. It had been kept secret from everybody. The theme was about forgetting things, and each teacher appeared before the headteacher, who was seated at his desk, to apologise for various mishaps. He pretended to rebuke each one and to tell them to be less forgetful in future. Finally, he arose to leave the stage and revealed he had 'forgotten' to put his trousers on. The audience was in fits of laughter, and we children were astonished to see our headmaster in his underpants.

Many years later, when I had just been appointed as a headteacher myself, I met the former head of that school in a corridor at the education office. I made myself known to him by saying, 'Hello Mr W; it's so nice to see you again, with your trousers on!'

By this time, he had moved into working in theatre himself, and he was amused to be reminded of this story and somewhat astonished to learn of my successful career.

I joined choirs at school, church and college, and, later, I joined choral groups with my husband. I loved singing and easily could be persuaded to perform at home when very small, as long as I could stand on the staircase out of sight. As an adult, I joined a local college musical society, and sang in a number of Gilbert and Sullivan productions – always as a 'chorus girl', which was great fun. We also sang *Orpheus in the Underworld*, and I joined in the cancan at every performance for a week, despite being pregnant with my first son. I loved the drama, costumes, greasepaint and 'ridiculousness' of it all.

A few years later, my first son (Shaun) and I took part in a musical at the Edinburgh Festival Fringe, and had a wonderful week with the rest of the cast, singing and dancing in the streets, as well as performing and singing to a mostly empty theatre each afternoon.

By contrast, in the week following the terrible tragedy at Dunblane School when many little children were gunned down by a man who was their scoutmaster, I sang a solo 'Pie Jesu' as part of the *Fauré Requiem* with a small choir, conducted by my husband. Many people in the audience were moved to tears as they reflected on the many little children who had lost their lives, and said how appropriate that piece of music had been. My membership as the first ever female in the choir was the result of all the choristers who were boys leaving in protest against the choirmaster, whom they disliked.

At my first service, the preacher announced, "Anita has joined the choir today. As you can tell we are desperate, so if anyone knows of any boys who would like to join please let the Choirmaster know."

One of my greatest pleasures has been to sing nursery songs to our little grandsons, who look at me in amazement when I join in with the actions to 'Wheels on the Bus', etc. William once gave me a good rendering of 'Let It Go' from the film *Frozen* with his toy guitar, a microphone and a swagger – he said he wants to be a rock star when he grows up.

My career with disabled children taught me many things, including children's universal love of music and mime.

<hr />

Church going during my childhood was obligatory since I 'belonged' to The Children's Society (formerly the Church of England Children's Society). I went to Sunday morning services and to Sunday school in Shirley church for all of my childhood. I hated the long services, where I sat in high, boxed pews from which I could see nothing and was made to sit still. However, I learned the hymns and rituals by heart, and have remained a committed churchgoer for the rest of my life, apart from for few years. I enjoy the music, prayers and peacefulness, as well as the friendships gained. I have a strong faith. There have been many times in my career when I have been faced with difficult situations, particularly in my job as headteacher, when I have sent up a prayer in the privacy of my office for help with what I had to do. Inspiration and courage have always come to me, sometimes in unexpected ways.

The relationships in the foster home deteriorated over the years. I rebelled against the increasing punishments, the unhappy atmosphere and long periods spent in a bedroom without my tea. It was a very lonely time. I used to horrify my children with the true story of how I was made to eat the carrots I refused at dinner for tea and for breakfast the next day, until I was sick. I did indulge my own children in their dislike of some foods and my eldest son still cannot eat cheese.

The Children's Society's welfare visitor called at the house about once a month. It was always a time I dreaded. I was only asked if I was happy in front of my foster mother, so I could not voice my unhappiness. Much was made of my rebelliousness. I was urged to be grateful for all that was done for me, and I was reminded what a lucky girl I was. My foster mother often told me how I had been saved from the back streets of London, and so I should learn to be grateful, have better manners and try to be a good girl. I am still trying on that front. My husband says it's a huge struggle.

CHAPTER EIGHT

Grammar School Days

WHEN I PASSED THE ELEVEN-PLUS EXAM IN 1957 AND gained a place at the local grammar school, I was given my first bicycle. I had long wanted a bike. I had learned to ride my friends' bikes when they let me have a go. I needed the bike to cycle up the lane to the main road, about a mile away, to catch the school bus to the Queen Elizabeth Grammar School in Ashbourne. On my first day, I set off proudly with my new satchel on my back. The lane rises steadily all the way, so coming back down was one long exhilarating freewheel. Other village children were going to the local secondary modern school at the same time, so we had races up and down the lane. One day we crashed into each other and my front wheel buckled. I walked home heavy-hearted. My bike was put in the shed, never to be repaired, and I had to walk the lane every day as punishment in all weathers.

Doris, by this time, had a part-time job and was not at home until 10pm each day. I was supposed to get my own meal and prepare something for her and Tom, as well as doing my homework and taking the two dogs for a walk. I was just twelve; I had a lot of homework to do, and I was very rebellious and not a little lonely.

Things went from bad to worse and the social worker was called. In her report, she wrote, "Things are not going too well between Mrs Shepherd (Doris) and Anita, who is not very happy. She returned from her holiday with Sandra, after 3 weeks. She told me she had not wanted to come back."

It was decided that I should become a boarder at the grammar school to relieve some of the tension in the household. I was not consulted and was meant to see this as a punishment for my bad behaviour. Interestingly, in this same welfare officer's report is the information that Tom thought I might be better off at boarding school, as Doris and I were always arguing. Tom taught me one good lesson at that time, which I have always remembered. I appealed to him once when Doris was giving me grief and he said, "The thing to do to avoid arguments is just don't answer her back; keep quiet."

This was very much the way he reacted to her haranguing him, and it was wise advice, though hard for me to keep to. It was the only time I ever remember him giving me advice.

However, boarding school was a very positive solution for me. I started at the boarding house in September 1958, and after some initial apprehension, I loved it.

As I was closing my suitcase on the evening before I departed for boarding school, Doris pushed a brown paper bag into my hand and said, "You might need these. You know what they are for." Inside the bag was a sanitary belt with hooks attached and a packet of pads. This was my only introduction to menstruation and sex education, and I did not understand how or when I would need these articles. Many parents were not at all good at talking about such things.

At boarding school, for the first time, I had friends of my own age around me and activities to engage in. In 1958, at the Mansion House, which was the girls' boarding house, I made new friends and at weekends we would chill out together, spend hours practising back combing our hair and hitching our skirts up as the fashions dictated, going window shopping, going out on supervised walks and trips, and chatting up the boys who boarded, who lived in the old grammar school building opposite – especially on Friday nights when we joined them for ballroom dancing. Being able to practise for sporting and musical competitions together gave us the edge over the rest of the school and made them envious of the boarders, who often won events.

Holiday times back with Doris were still very difficult. I had no contact with my friends and was made to go to the village where her widowed stepmother lived, to keep her stepmother company in the holidays; I was lonely and rebellious.

During term time, the daily routine at the boarding house was breakfast at 8am – the smell and taste of burned toast and scrambled eggs still haunts me – followed by a fifteen-minute walk through the town to school. We boarders returned to the boys' school house at 12pm for lunch, returning for afternoon school at 1.30pm – it seemed a lot of walking.

Along the way, I had to pass a junction where Doris's friend managed a small tobacconist's shop. On days when Doris was working on her insurance collection job, she would join her friend for a natter. I began to realise that this occurred at precisely the time I would be walking to and from school for lunch or back at teatime. The two of them would stand at the open shop door, and appeared to be laughing at me and making derogatory comments about my appearance, which Doris commented on whenever I went home for a holiday. I was extremely unhappy and embarrassed.

Sometimes my friends would say, "Who are those two women pointing at you over there?" or, worse, "Is that your mother?"

I was mortified.

My daily walks to and from school were agony. I began to find an alternative route, which was longer but out of her view, until I arrived at school late and was reprimanded by the boarding school housemother who soon got to know about it. Again, I was unable to tell her the true reason, since I had no idea that she would know about my home circumstances. I had a great fear of authority figures and what they might do to me. It stemmed from my fear of being 'sent away and locked up' whenever I misbehaved.

I was always interested in boys at school. When I was fourteen, I became aware that one of the boys at the boarding house liked me, and I really liked him. We sat next to each other whenever we could, held hands on the way to school and escaped on country walks during free times at weekends. It was an innocent but intense relationship for me. My first time falling in love and knowing those intense, sweet feelings of being close to someone who cared about me, but we were not alone in private often. One day, he shyly presented me with a present in a small box. It was a pretty brooch. It wasn't my birthday, and this came completely out of the blue. I was thrilled – it was my first present from my boyfriend.

Some days later, the headmaster's wife, our housemother, called me into the study, looked me in the eye and said, not unkindly, "Anita, where is the brooch? Please fetch it at once. I know all about it."

I was mortified. I wondered how she had found out about it and why it was obviously viewed with much anger. I fetched the brooch from my bedside drawer and, shamefaced, I gave it to her.

She said, "I shall say no more about this, but I do not want to hear of you walking to and from school with the boys. You are too young for that kind of thing. I shall be watching. Now run along, dear, and get ready for supper."

How times have changed.

The next day, I tried in vain to catch my boyfriend's eye. I wanted to know about the brooch and why it had been taken from me. He avoided me, and it became clear that we were no longer together. I cried my eyes out in silence in bed. It was a very unhappy experience, and revived all my feelings about rejection and loss. Many years later, I bumped into a man who had been at the boarding house at that time. He was quick to remind me about the brooch incident, and the truth was finally revealed. A boy who was friendly with my boyfriend had stolen the brooch from the counter at the Woolworth's store in the town and had given it to him as a present for me. The police were called as the staff at the store recognised the boy, who had been stealing regularly. He was duly expelled, but I never knew the connection at the time.

During my school years, I developed an interest in classical music. It started when, at the boarding house, a girl played a record on the gramophone over and over again. It was a violin concerto by Bruch. I was moved deeply by its haunting melodies. Until that time, I had only been aware of music's powerful effect from the radio programmes played back at home in the background. Like all teenagers, I loved pop tunes and the scratchy sounds that came out of someone's transistor radio under the bedcovers in the dormitory. If discovered, the 'tranny' was confiscated and we all had to get up at ridiculous o'clock to write lines saying, "I must not listen to music in bed." Or worse, if we were caught talking late after lights out we might be woken at 6am to write out long passages from the *Financial Times* – in complete silence – which were handed in then torn up and thrown away immediately.

Our music teacher at the grammar school was Chris. His room was at the top of the three-storey tower block. As a teacher, he seemed to have it dead easy. We would tramp up to his 'lair' and, as an introduction to the lesson, he would say, "Sit down, shut up and listen."

He would put on a record of a piece of classical music with the minimum of introduction, sit himself down, light his pipe and read his paper. The music always finished, or was ended, just in time for him to give us homework – usually a critique of the piece of music and something about the composer. In the days without the internet, that research was a tall order for most of us. In the first two years of compulsory music, that was all that was required of him to excite us with the desire to drop geography and listen to such classics as *Scheherazade* by Rimsky-Korsakov (or 'Corsets-off', as the boys liked to joke) for another three years or more. He had a good sense of humour mixed with a laid-back approach to learning, which was much appreciated by the non-musical pupils. I began to have violin lessons, and I joined the school choir.

Mr Atkinson asked me one day if I would like to change from learning the violin to the cello, as the school had an instrument spare and no one to play it. It now seems to me a poor reason for choosing a 'budding musician', but as I was not enjoying the violin it was an easy decision. He was not a cellist himself, but taught me the basics in a very thorough way. I studied cello with him for four years, and I even played in the school orchestra. When I left school, there was no one to buy a cello for me or pay for lessons, so I didn't play again for a very long time.

Many years later, my husband, John and I were on holiday in Prague. We share a great love of music and we went to a number of concerts. At one, a quartet was playing, and I could not take my eyes off the cellist.

John, who was watching me, said, "Have you ever thought of taking up the cello again?"

In the wink of an eye, I said, "No, but, yes, I'd like to!" and so my second age of cello playing began. With a hired cello, I found that I could remember much of what I had learned over thirty years before. and my husband took me to Edinburgh where we purchased a fine, new cello – made in China – with a bright, lively tone. I found a great young teacher. I'm still playing, off and on, learning from a book entitled *I Used to Play Cello*.

In 1970, when I returned to Ashbourne to work, Chris met me in the street. He looked at my then five-year-old son David, and said, "When is he joining the church choir then?"

I felt compelled to let David join. I was a proud mum when I watched him singing in church. I think he enjoyed the company of the other boys for a while. I never heard him sing at any other time – he always refused to sing at home. Eventually, Sunday football games competed for my son's attendance, and, despite weekly nagging by Chris, David chose football. My new partner at that time, John – himself an organist and choirmaster – joined the church choir about the same time, which helped Chris to overlook my son's departure. Chris died in 1992, and another choirmaster took over the role. He did not have Chris's humour and good relationship with the boys, and they all left within a month. The church was in a quandary – it had possessed a male choir with men and boys only for many generations. There was a public meeting about inviting 'females' to join.

"Over my dead body," said the new choirmaster.

Within a few weeks the choirmaster asked John if he thought I would help out as there were no soprano voices, and the repertoire was extensive. After some deliberating, because my life was already busy, I agreed to try.

At the first evening service when I put on a cassock and sang, the elderly clergyman announced from the pulpit, "Anita has joined the choir today. As you can see we are desperate for singers so if you know any boys that would like to sing…"

There was much giggling in the choir at that.

Becoming a member of the church choir in Ashbourne gave me huge pleasure. Rehearsals can seem arduous, but performing great music together was thrilling to me. I have learned hundreds of anthems and psalms over the past twenty years, and improved my ability to read music. There is a feeling of tremendous friendship and warmth in this and other communities of singers. I sang with them for thirteen years before my voice became unstable and I retired. Nowadays, the choir singing each Sunday is comprised mostly of women!

─── ⌘ ───

We all have memorable teachers who inspired us and gave us a love of a particular subject. I enjoyed English and French lessons especially, and found I had an ability to speak a language quite easily. Maths was another thing all together. As I have previously mentioned, I have struggled with maths all my life. When I got to my first maths lesson at grammar school, it was apparent to me immediately that I would have to apply all this unknown knowledge to very taxing questions.

The teacher was a first-class mathematician whose approach to teaching the less able – that is, me – was to say, "Come up to the blackboard, Anita," in a friendly tone. Then he would hand me a piece of chalk and say, "Show us how to work it out."

I had no idea. The resulting shame, fear and blushing cheeks were to haunt me every Monday morning at maths lessons. I used to dream that I had missed all my maths lessons for a whole year and failed the exams, which I did eventually. On one exam paper, I merely wrote my name and stared blankly out of the window. I hated that feeling of not understanding. It certainly gave me insights for later years when I worked with adults who could not read or write.

Toward the end of my fourth year as a boarder at the school, Doris started to put pressure on me to leave the boarding house and become a day pupil again. She told me how unhappy I seemed as I walked between buildings at school, that I always looked so miserable, that she was concerned for me and that was why she looked out for me. I protested that this was not so, but she kept on at me. I did not trust her, but could find no strong defence. She did not suggest that I was missed at home or that she cared about me. It was a very bleak time for me. She promised to have my bedroom decorated and that she would buy me a new dressing table with drapes, which she thought I would like. I now suspect that the loss of income for fostering me was an issue for her since Tom's salary was not great.

Recently, I chatted to a man at the airport as we waited for our gate number to be called. It emerged that he had also grown up in Shirley village, about the same time as me.

"Where did you live?" he asked.

When I mentioned Tom and Doris he smiled and said, "Tom was a true gentleman. Everybody knew and liked him. He only had one fault – he was always slow in collecting his money."

He went on to say that he often chased Tom up the lane asking for a bill.

Tom would always reply, "Oh aye, I must get round to working it out."

Even after his retirement, money was still outstanding from many of his customers.

When I continued to refuse stubbornly when Doris nagged me to come home, she changed tack and said she could not afford to keep me at boarding school with all the costs (I did not know at that time that The Children's Society were funding me). She went on and on. I felt I had no one to talk to.

During the school holidays, she would return home from her job at 10pm, come into my room, switch on the light, shake me awake and then begin again with the same arguments. Whether she genuinely believed I would be happier at home, I do not know. She had never asked me about my life at school, so could not have known how I felt. Eventually, she wore me down and I gave in.

The following September, with heavy heart I returned to being a day pupil. It was agony explaining to my friends what had happened. I avoided my former pals because of this and surely gained a reputation as being stuck up. I regret my lack of courage in speaking out about my situation.

CHAPTER NINE

A Break Away

DURING THE 1961 SUMMER HOLIDAYS, I WENT ON AN exchange holiday to France to stay with a French girl and her family. The Children's Society had agreed to fund this, and arrangements were made through the kindness of my school's headmaster and his wife. Doris was furious when she found out that I would be away for a month of the school's summer holidays. She was forced to agree to buy clothes for my trip, but took no joy in my preparations.

I first went by train to London and was met by a social worker from The Children's Society, who was to take me across the city to meet a coach to take me to the airport. I was very excited and nervous to be travelling abroad, and to be journeying alone by train and then plane. The friendly woman and I travelled to a building in Kennington, which was the headquarters of The Children's Society. We went into the building, and I remember there being long, dark corridors and staircases. I was left outside an office whilst she went in to fetch her papers, and we left after a very short time. I was to be reminded of this part of my journey years later, and apprised of some devastating details.

My trip to France was wonderful. I went alone by small plane to Beauvais. I stayed in Paris for a few days with my penfriend, Odile, together with her relatives. I particularly recall an evening riding in an open-topped car with other teenagers and their uncle around the sights of Paris – the Champs-Élysée, the Eiffel Tower, etc. The sights were lit with twinkling lights, and there were several lanes of speeding traffic and noise. I was spellbound and in heaven. I loved the freedom. It was great to be with other young people.

Later, we travelled by night train through France to the Gironde area. We were met by Odile's family and taken to their farm. Peaches were produced in orchards stretching for miles. All family members, including the youngsters, helped to pick and grade the fruit. Discovering I could eat as many peaches as I wanted, I made myself very unwell and spent the next day on a very primitive toilet, just like the one back at home used to be. The other teenagers thought it a huge joke.

We had many wonderful adventures. No one spoke English, so I had no choice but to speak their language, and I improved my spoken French a lot. We had a trip to see the cave paintings at Lascaux, which were amazing – especially so when I knew a little more history as I grew older. The caves were closed to the public a few years later because of potential damage from so many visitors.

My month with them all passed too quickly and I returned to England, Shirley village and Doris with a heavy heart and rebellion on my mind. We clashed immediately. She did not want to hear about my wonderful trip. I had got the travel bug.

———

Doris's next notion was to persuade me to leave school after taking O levels, and to find work. She was so determined that she even got an interview for me as a receptionist at a company in Ashbourne. I went along for the interview, knowing nothing and with no enthusiasm. I was offered the job.

I saw an advert in the local paper for school leavers to apply to train to work with disabled children. I was more enthusiastic about this opportunity and wrote for an application form. I had to put my headmaster's name for a reference.

The headmaster of my school, a very kind but distant man, sent for me. He said, "Anita, I hear you are thinking of leaving school at the end of term."

I explained about the opportunity to train to teach disabled children. Sadly, I felt unable to explain about Doris's resistance to me staying on into the sixth form. I had no confidence in my ability to study at university.

He looked at me in silence for a while, then said, "I am very sorry to hear that. You have done well. We expect you to stay on to the sixth form, and you should aim for university. You could study English or French, as you have done well in both those subjects. You must understand that you will never make a successful career out of that kind of work."

"I am sorry; I have to leave and I want do this," I replied lamely.

He wished me good luck with a certain sadness. I was unaware that he and most of my teachers knew of the problems I faced in the foster home. Sadly, I was too ashamed to try to unburden myself to them and nobody ever broached the subject with me. How I wish I could have told him just how successful and fulfilling my career working with disabled children became eventually.

Just at the end of my last term in school, when I was nearly seventeen, I met a man who would become my first husband. He was twenty-four, lively and very funny. He was a painter and decorator, and he had a black Ford Zephyr car, which he was immensely proud of. He asked me out for a date. I had a difficult time persuading Doris, but she let me go because another girl from school would be there too.

We began a regular friendship, and I met his family and went on holiday with them. I fell in love with the first person who had ever shown me affection. I had no idea about relationships with men, and I had no role model and no one to talk to about marriage. I badly needed love and a home not a Home.

About this time, I decided to write to the social worker who visited me to tell her my side of the story. I didn't think through what the consequences might be. I sketched out some thoughts about how I felt unloved, criticised, demeaned and dismissed by my foster mother. I bought some notepaper and envelopes secretly, ready to write and send the letter. This was my undoing. Doris found the envelopes and looked for the notes. She said nothing to me, though her mood was thunderous for the next couple of days. She had sent for the social worker on reading my notes; the social worker arrived, and I was ordered to my bedroom whilst they talked about me.

Eventually, the social worker called me downstairs. No mention was made about the notes; she simply said, "Anita, go upstairs and pack your clothes."

I well remember standing in the room that had been my bedroom for the last ten years and wondering what, if anything in it, was really mine. Doris knew I was determined to go my own way, and she had me removed to a children's home in Ashbourne for a brief spell. I was then sixteen years old. The whole of this period was extremely stressful for me, and I had only my boyfriend to turn to. He was a very happy-go-lucky kind of man, teasing and confident, never worried and quite irresponsible at times, enjoying meeting his mates and socialising. He was incredibly kind and helpful to me in all that I attempted over the next few years. He was very accepting of my strange circumstances, but I never discussed with him any of the traumas I had gone through. I was sure he would not understand. I became very independent – a trait that has sometimes caused me some problems, since I know I am not easy to live with. Life with my foster parents ceased to be relevant, and I saw them very infrequently for the next couple of years, although Doris again sought me out to try to persuade me to return.

CHAPTER TEN

A New Beginning

WHEN I STARTED A PROBATIONARY PERIOD OF WORK IN September 1962, I was sent to a modern day centre in a small town some distance from Shirley. I had to find accommodation in the area during the week, because I had nowhere else to live. This first experience set the pattern of working with disabled children for the rest of my life; I loved it and poured all my energies and skills into it. I found it easy to put my past behind me. Every day was challenging, fun and exhausting. The adults there were much older than me and very kind.

I moved to my second placement in another day centre in an old church hall near Derby in January 1963, and I went to live with my boyfriend's sister Joyce, her husband Dennis and their young family. They made me very welcome and treated me like an adult. I was free to go out, and spend time with my boyfriend and his friends. The Children's Society was still responsible for me, so Joyce and Dennis had to be vetted, and they had to report on me from time to time. Their home was a very positive and friendly environment to live in and I was happy. Their daughter, Linda, then just two years of age, grew up very close to me and, eventually, was influenced to choose a career working with disabled children. She became a qualified teacher many years later and, in due course, was employed at the school at which I had been the headteacher. This link has always meant a lot to me. Her brother became friendly with my son Shaun as they grew up, and they still spend time together on holidays.

My foster mother was difficult every time I went to back to see her as an independent woman, and I gradually 'broke free' and saw less of her. She was, I think, very jealous of my new-found family and probably missed me, though she would never admit to that. If other people praised my successes, she would dismiss them out of hand.

My third placement that year was in a disused library in Alfreton, a town some ten miles from where I was living. I learned such a lot during that year and knew by the end of the summer that this was definitely what I wanted to do more than anything else. With a new family to support and encourage me, I began to gain confidence and did not feel so alone any more. I saw a very different side to normal family life and discovered that throwing all my energies into my job left no time to dwell on my past life. Though the work was challenging, it was a very happy period for me.

Many years later, encouraged by my counsellor, I wrote to The Children's Society, and a welfare officer from The Children's Society came to Derby to see me. I was keen to find out about my father. The welfare officer informed me that current legislation did not allow for information about him to be revealed unless he was asking about my sister and me. The records and reports about my childhood proved interesting, and revealed to me how many people knew what was happening to me when I was growing up. I had felt so entirely alone. More importantly, they confirmed the breakdown of my relationship with my foster parents. Nowadays, I am sure there would be much closer discussion with a child in this situation. I have, however, a unique record of reports about my progress throughout my childhood.

I learned in the summer of 1963 that I was to be seconded by the county council to a teacher training course in Bristol. This was the start of an exciting new phase in my life. When I was due to go to college, a social worker took me out to buy new clothes, and I got my first duffle coat, in dark green. It was very fashionable at the time. It was almost my last regular contact with social workers, who ceased responsibility for my welfare when I became eighteen.

The training course was not affiliated with any local college but rather to the National Association for Teachers of Mentally Handicapped Children, as it was then called. Tutors had a free hand to deliver a curriculum that was highly original and unusual. Instead of spending time studying the theories and history of education, we underwent a hands-on, creative programme to develop our skills in working with children with multiple disabilities. At that time, little was known about the development of learning in such children. Much was made of developing our observational ability to discern what children were trying to say and do. It became clear that the children were certainly very individual; they each wanted to engage with their surroundings, and many strived to communicate in some way. Around all of that were their very individual personalities.

I lived in an hostel for international students from all over the world, which was a great experience for me. I was attached to a family with a young boy with Down's syndrome, from whom I learned a lot about family life. I had a great time. I received my diploma in 1965 and returned to Derbyshire to get married.

Part Two

CHAPTER ELEVEN

A 'Mentally Handicapped Teacher'

"Have another baby and you will soon forget about this one." This incredible advice has often been quoted to me by parents of disabled babies as the only suggestion they received from medical professionals when their baby's condition was diagnosed.

I do believe in fate or perhaps it was divine intervention that led me to what became a long career working with disabled children. I had no personal experience of disability or of children with problems, except to be aware of a boy in the village who never went to school and who wandered about the lanes talking to himself. I was, and am, passionately fond of children, and I love their company. In my career, I developed an intuitive understanding of the difficulties that disabled children have and of what they are trying to say. I can identify with those who struggle with life, and it has given me great joy to work with them. My career helped me to put aside the harsh experiences I had in childhood and concentrate wholly on finding out how to help disadvantaged children.

The fate of children born with physical or mental disabilities before the 1950s was dire. Parents were often told at birth that the children would never be 'normal' and would probably not reach adulthood. They were advised to put the child into care and forget about it. Their child was certified as ineducable, and headteachers of mainstream schools could not accept them. Imagine receiving that prognosis as a new parent.

Babies born with severe physical deformities were frequently placed in 'subnormality hospitals' early on in their lives, often located far away from their families and their home environment in austere, locked wards in large, remote country houses. There many remained for the rest of their lives. My visits to such hospitals during my training left me traumatised – I could not believe that such a system existed, although the people working in the hospitals were heroic in their attempts to make the children and young adults' lives interesting without any resources to do so.

Those children who remained at home were often unseen by society. The social stigma was huge, and parents and families were quick to blame some aspect of either family's history or behaviour for the child's condition. Mothers anguished about things that happened in pregnancy, which they believed could have caused the disablement; the Thalidomide scare in the 1960s reinforced this idea.

There was no advice for new parents as they struggled with feeding difficulties, fits, sickness, and exhaustion from lack of sleep and from carrying a heavy child around.

Such children were labelled by the medical profession with the most grotesque labels: idiot, imbecile, cretin, mental defective and mongol. These awful labels actually denoted to the medical professions the perceived degree of mental backwardness.

Parents often suffered prejudice from others too. Well-meaning folk looking in the pram at the new baby did not know what to say and their lack of words was agony for some parents. Others never took their child out where there might be hostility. Information about normal developmental delay was in its infancy.

When I began taking small groups of pupils out in the town during my later career, in the early 1970s, I was faced with unkind comments from members of the public such as, "Those children should not be allowed out."

Like most people working in this field, I felt I often had a responsibility to educate the general public to see these children as worthy of living a normal life. People are often afraid of what they do not understand; prejudice about disability has been very hard to combat over the decades, and it's still a problem today.

There was no statutory day care provided for these children before the 1950s, and parents just had to cope alone. Across the country, an embryonic association of parents of 'mentally handicapped children' was developing, with support from a few national figures that had personal experiences of severe disabilities. Thus Mencap was born, and it still leads the field in promoting the development of services for children and adults.

Initially, some parents came together in local community or church halls to provide some day facilities where mums and children could meet together. This sharing of knowledge has been a catalyst for changing society's attitudes toward children and adults with significant learning problems.

Terminology has always been difficult. Society loves labels, but parents just want their child to be treated as normal – whatever that means. Each generation has tried to find better ways of identifying children's medical and social conditions for total access to local mainstream schools, and debates still rage about respectable terminology. Thanks to parents pressuring the government, by January 1971, disabled children formerly excluded from schools were finally able to access their local schools and the 'exclusion because of disability' stigma was abolished. Many parents hoped for a new world in which their child could go to school with their brothers and sisters, be able to make friends there, and be fully integrated into school life. The reality for many children has been much different and more complicated than anyone imagined.

Although I had no children of my own when I began working in day centres, I recognised the sadness of parents who had gone through pregnancy, looked forward to their baby's arrival, given birth in all its pain, only to be faced with the devastation of their child being less than they expected. Or, sometimes, the lovely baby seemed complete at birth but failed to make normal progress in the milestones of walking, talking and feeding. Parents would become increasingly anxious, seek advice from family and friends, and mention to their doctor reluctantly that they thought something might be wrong with their child. Disabilities sometimes appear little by little, as with autism, and parents' worries are increased.

Recently, I spoke to a nurse who was taking a blood sample from me. She revealed that she has a teenage autistic son and has great fears for his future. She said to me, "To be honest, we almost hope that he will go before us, because he would never cope if we were not around. Even my own mother won't acknowledge him."

CHAPTER TWELVE

Starting Work

WHEN I WAS EMPLOYED BY THE LOCAL AUTHORITY IN 1962, they had a duty to provide some day care for the children described as 'ineducable' through their mental health service. Day centres were organised in a variety of locations around the country, primarily to give some relief to families. There was little government funding for such work, and the activities at the centres were not well defined.

My first job was as a trainee mental health supervisor. The term 'teacher' could not be used because we did not fit into the statutory education category, nor were we qualified to teach in schools. My first placement was in a small industrial town in South East Derbyshire, at a newly built day centre, which was unique at that time. It was a light, airy building with excellent facilities for the children, who were aged two to eighteen years.

The focus of activity was on keeping the children occupied, happy and well behaved, whilst engaging them in practical craftwork activities, which could lead to sales to parents and income for the local mental health authority services. This seems an incredible idea nowadays. Most days, after the children had gone home, we adults were required to unpick the craft items and redo them so they were fit for sale as 'items made by the children'.

That first day was a memorable experience. I was excited and anxious in equal measure. I had no idea how I would react to the children, or they to me. I was straight out of school and felt I knew nothing, except that I had a great love of children. I arrived very early and waited for the arrival of the buses and taxis that brought the children in from a wide area. I held my breath as soon the front doors burst open, and in charged a small person with a huge smile who grabbed my hand and said, "Hello. You my friend?"

I was smitten, and remained so for the next 30 years of my career.

I found it easy to 'get down to the children's level', literally, and – with care – listen to their halting speech and talk to them in simple language, not using baby talk. I discovered how to give them instructions and share information in bite-sized chunks, which became a guiding principle for me in this work.

I soon discovered, to my amazement, the range of personalities that shone through, whatever the difficulties. Some children were lively, restless, cheeky and interested in their surroundings. Others were shy, quiet, spoke rarely, and needed lots of reassurance and encouragement. Some seemed locked in a world of their own, with little ability to communicate or react. With guidance from the other adults, I learned to understand their individual personalities and difficulties, and to be imaginative in helping them overcome them. Many had medical problems that are more fully understood today. I learned the important lesson that children are just children, but that these had more difficulties in understanding the world than most of us.

There was a lot of humour and banter from the children, as well as the staff, who were a team of dedicated, down-to-earth women. I was the youngest and I had so much to learn. We had no national curriculum, no teaching resources and no computers; we instructed, played and cared intuitively, and did lots of singing and fun games – it was just up my street. We worked hard to give the children confidence and social skills, and to improve their ability to communicate with us and others. All of them, without exception, loved music – to listen to, to try to sing to and, best of all, to make their own sounds with a range of home-made percussion instruments.

There was so little around to guide us as to best practice. I was enthusiastic and caring, but very ignorant of how to help them develop – or how far they might progress. We had no help from speech therapists, occupational therapists, psychologists or any of the many experts who would regularly give support in a modern school – that was all many years away for us – so we did our best to love and to care for each fragile soul.

Later, I was involved in working within the homes of disabled teenagers and adults who had never received any kind of help with their educational needs, but had lived at home with their parents all their lives. My role was to listen, give some ideas for occupying and managing their child, and if possible, take him or her out into the community to give their parents a break. This gave me huge insights into the many difficult issues for parents, not least the stigma of having such a child in the family. I began to hear the often-repeated plea, "What will happen to him/her when we are gone?" This knowledge was the foundation for my approach to parents when I became a headteacher later in my career.

After one school term, I was sent to another centre nearer to the city of Derby. This was in a church hall with no suitable facilities for children. It had a rough, wooden floor and metal cupboards that had to house every bit of our equipment at the end of every day. There were no small chairs, toilets or basins for the little ones. Changing nappies was a nightmare, and holding the little ones on the adult toilet reminded me of my childhood fear of the outside loo. There were folding metal chairs and tables that had to be stacked in a corridor each evening and brought out every morning before the children arrived. The hall was situated alongside a very busy main road, and there were no safety gates on the drive. Ensuring that the 'runners' amongst our children could not dash out of the door was one person's responsibility. The head supervisor's 'office' was in one of three metal cupboards at the end of the main room, and whenever the telephone rang one of the children would yell, "Phone, sush everybody!" Privacy was non-existent.

It was a useful experience for me in a number of ways. I developed an acute awareness of how individual and unique each child was, and how they functioned, how they saw the world and what difficulties they had with ordinary, everyday tasks. I never saw them according to a label. Many of the young people had a sense of humour; they liked to be amused and could tease others. Some struggled hard to communicate. Others were often angry, probably because they could not communicate. Most functioned like much younger children. I learned a lot about showing love and compassion, which was strange since I didn't have much experience of those qualities in my own life. Perhaps all of my need for affection was channelled into these young people. This was all without feeling sad about whatever the children could not do at any one time – building on the positive always.

Music has always motivated me, and I quickly built up a repertoire of songs, nursery rhymes, etc. I still know all the words and actions to 'The Wheels on the Bus' and 'I Can Sing a Rainbow' is etched on my mind as the song that all the disabled children I ever encountered wanted to sing.

I longed to add to my knowledge of how the children functioned, what their disabling conditions meant for them and how we could alleviate some of their problems. Having fun was always my first priority with the children. They usually accepted everything that happened to them without complaint.

My third term was based at a centre housed in an old library building next to a busy main road in another small town on the edge of major coalfields. I never discovered why this building was used as a day centre, as it was entirely unsuited to the needs of children let alone those with multiple learning and physical difficulties.

School dinners would arrive at midday in huge metal 'canteens', and were often lukewarm and unappetising. Feeding children in such difficult and cramped rooms – under the main library building – next to a coke boiler was quite an experience.

One teenager, who had been blind from birth through lack of oxygen, sticks in my mind. I will call him George. He lived in a village with his elderly, widowed mother and her sister. He was an attractive boy, who was aged twelve at that time, and was tall, with beautiful auburn hair and sightless blue eyes. His behaviour was disruptive and demanding. He needed constant attention, although he could talk well, and was physically able to move about and negotiate the furniture. George talked to himself incessantly and walked on his toes. Knowing his home circumstances, and with my experiences of working with families, I was asked to visit his home. George's mum, who was a widow living with her sister, welcomed me and was pleased to have his 'teacher' to talk to. George spent the whole time as we talked pulling his mother's hair and forcing her face away from me toward his. He was physically strong. She told me that he insisted on sleeping in the same bed with her and disrupted her sleep most nights. His distressed mother showed me several bruises she had from his obsessive behaviour, and said she was, "at the end of her tether". She asked me what would happen to him when she was no longer around.

Gently, I broached the subject of respite care, and suggested that it could be like a holiday for him, as well as a rest for her and her elderly sister, and that it would be good for him to be with young people of his own age.

Immediately, she said, "Oh no, I couldn't send him away."

I tried to persuade her to think that it might be something her son would enjoy – being with other young people – but to no avail. She believed no one else could care for him properly and that he would be lost without her.

A few years passed and I moved on to another place. I heard that both George's mother and sister had died in the same year. George had to go immediately as an emergency admission into a mental hospital.

Within a few months, he had died too. He never adjusted to the loss of his mother. I felt sad at this news. The issues around parents 'letting go' and accepting care away from home were to be a constant subject raised with me throughout my career.

That year's experience was very important to me and confirmed in my heart that this was the work I was meant for. I never could have imagined how far the education of children like these would progress in the future, but I was always convinced that we should not put up barriers to their opportunities in life, but should help them to achieve whatever they desired. They have rights like everybody else.

CHAPTER THIRTEEN

College Life
and Wedding Bells

DURING THE SUMMER OF 1963, I LEARNED THAT I HAD BEEN
successful in achieving a place on a teacher training course in
Bristol to study for a diploma for teachers of mentally handicapped
children, which was one of only three such courses in the country
at that time and the only recognised qualification. I was sponsored
by the county council with the obligation that I must return to
work for them for at least two years after qualifying. At that time,
there were no courses for people working in day centres with
these children. An independent body, the National Association for
Mentally Handicapped Teachers (NAMHT) was established in the
early 1960s and provided a year's training. This became a two-year
diploma course, which I joined with four other young women from
Derbyshire in September 1963.

This was the start of an exciting new phase in my life. The
Children's Society sent a social worker to see me, who took me out to
buy new clothes, and I got my first duffle coat – in dark green – and a
college scarf, which was fashionable at the time. It was almost my last
regular contact with social workers, who ceased responsibility for my
welfare when I reached eighteen. The Children's Society contributed

toward my accommodation costs whilst I was at college, and my social worker was kept informed by the college tutors about my progress. Once again, I had no idea that any one was looking out for me.

———⁕———

My move to Bristol was exciting but scary. I had been living in digs in Derby with a family for the past year, but had hardly ever travelled away from Derbyshire apart from my trip to France to stay with a penfriend. I suppose I felt like all teenagers living in a strange city for the first time. I had a boyfriend back in Derby who was anxious that I might find someone else, and was urging me to go back to Derby to see him every weekend and holiday.

Bristol is a beautiful city, especially for students, and I enjoyed my time there. Our base was in another old church property, which was a large Georgian house. The training course was outstandingly innovative for its time. Our lead tutor was an inspiration. She taught us to understand child development in relation to disabled children through a lot of 'holistic experiences'. We organised a weekly play group for 'normal' and disabled children together, in the college rooms. We were each linked to a family throughout the course, to carry out a longitudinal study of the effects on the family of having such a child. We had a tutor for physical education, and movement and dance, Veronica Sherbourne, who was a charismatic teacher with novel ideas about how to encourage children to be more mobile, confident and independent. "Use your body as a climbing frame for little ones" was one of her mantras. Children who had little control of their limbs or could not walk were placed on the back of a student kneeling on the floor, and we would move and sway to music to give the child experience of a different kind of moving and being transported. It was also incredibly calming for hyperactive children.

When he was small, I heard my agile grandson, William, saying, "Come on, Daddy, get down!" He wanted to use his daddy for a climbing frame. My thoughts went back to those distant days of crawling around a church hall with a floppy child on my back, with delight on his/her face. What a lovely memory. With a tuneable tambour Veronica would beat out rhythms for the children to copy on the floor or against our backs. She had a deep understanding of and empathy for these children. She went on to become known internationally for her work, and I was privileged to attend two of her workshops around the country in later years.

When she saw me, trying to recall who I was, she said, "Ah, you were in one of the first groups I taught. I've learned so much since then."

She was a truly inspiring teacher.

Whilst I was on my first teaching practice at a day centre in a town near to the college, I had another awful experience involving a man. It happened like this. A man appeared in the classroom I was working in. I was actually in the garden of the nursery, playing with two little ones. I was introduced to the man by the teacher. I shall call him 'Henry'. He was a mental health social worker. His role was working with families of disabled children within the city. He must have been about forty-five at that time. He offered to give me a lift back to my hostel in the city, and I accepted since the teacher seemed to know him well.

The following day he was outside my college gate when I left with friends, and he beckoned me over and said, "I was just passing and thought you might like a lift."

"No, thanks; I don't want to trouble you. I'll walk," I replied.

"It's no trouble."

To avoid a tricky scene, as other students were around, I accepted. He then stalked me every day for several weeks. It seemed that wherever I was, whatever the time, he would be outside waiting. I began to feel anxious throughout my day in case he appeared. I told him I preferred to walk with my friends. They were beginning to ask about him and look at me in a strange way. Finally, one day he waited for me on my walk home after I had left my friends. He opened his car door and ordered me into his car. There was a brief argument, coaxing and persuasion, and I somehow found myself in his car not wanting to make a scene. I thought my obvious distress would make him realise that I wanted to go straight back to my lodgings. How little I knew; how naïve I was. He drove out of the city, away from my hostel.

"Where are we going?" I asked, "I have to get back; just drop me off and I will walk."

"I thought you might like a little trip. There's no need to worry; I'll be only a few minutes then you will be back," he explained.

He sped on, saying he just had to pop home for some papers and somehow we arrived at his house. I was persuaded to go in and meet his wife. This story seems bizarre when told now. His wife was not there and he quickly forced his wet, slobbering lips against my mouth and pushed me into a bedroom. He raped me. I remember struggling, biting his hand, desperately trying to keep my clothes around my legs, protesting and squealing. But it was to no avail. Afterwards, he arranged his clothes calmly, handed me a tissue; smiled and said, "You are good"; and opened the front door to leave. He drove me back to my hostel in the city, calm and chatty, seemingly oblivious to me shaking and crying beside him.

I still don't know why I never told anyone about all this. I was so ashamed to have been so easily manipulated. I could not believe that someone who seemed so old to me should want to attack me in this way. I had given him no encouragement. I felt dirty, so lonely and sick in my heart. We never heard of such things in the press. Sex was scarcely talked about, even with friends. Much later in my life, I sought counselling to remove this awful guilt from my heart, and I now see that power and control are the things that drive such men, and it that was not my fault. It affected my view of men greatly. I never saw him again. He knew I had stayed in contact with the class teacher, and he was possibly worried that I would tell her. I had threatened to do so, but she became ill at the same time, and I felt I could not add to her worries.

Now, many decades later when stories of abusers are in every newspaper and celebrities are in court, I know that my experience was and still is all too common. Several close women friends have shared similar experiences with me. I never thought of going to the police, as I believed I would not be understood, which is probably true. I felt a deep sense of shame. I never told anyone – not my boyfriend or anyone else – about this incident, and, like so many other traumas in my life, I put it out of my mind and moved on. I am so glad that society and the police take these issues more seriously these days, and believe what has happened when a girl or adult woman reports it. This would not have been the case in 1964. It is still a harrowing experience, and I fear I would not have been able to cope with describing to a policeman what had happened; after all, students were presumed to be promiscuous, weren't they? This was the 1960s with all its presumed freedom. The many cases in the news in recent years and the 'Me Too' movement have stirred up these memories, which I had pushed out of my mind, and it has had an effect on my health as well as my relationships. My husband John is the first person I have ever spoken to about this event, and not until I was sixty years old.

My sister, Sandra, meanwhile, was trying to adjust to being part of an adoptive family in rural Cumbria. She had experienced ten different foster homes in her first few years, and was a very disturbed child. Her adoptive parents were good, kindly people. They had no other children. They ran a village shop and post office, and had a busy life. Sandra was often in conflict with her adoptive mother, who had rigid ideas about how Sandra should behave. By her mid-teens, Sandra was pregnant. Her parents sent her away from the village to a home for fallen girls whilst she waited for the baby to be born. The regime in the home was strict and punitive, and Sandra was very unhappy. In 1964, she gave birth to a beautiful girl, Dawn. Ironically, Sandra was then allowed to return home and her baby was shown proudly to all the villagers who came into the post office. Matters within the household deteriorated, and Sandra decided to leave. Her parents would not allow her to take her baby with her and, eventually, they adopted Dawn, their grandchild, and brought her up as their own child. I knew nothing of all this until many years had passed.

I passed my exams at the end of the second year, got my diploma for teachers of the mentally handicapped, and returned to Derbyshire to get married and start a new career.

My wedding day passed in a blur of 'this is not happening to me'. I already suspected that we would not be compatible. I had begun to see that I was marrying a man who shirked responsibility and wanted to have a good time. I had no idea what a lifelong commitment really meant, and the example of a happy home was something I had not experienced throughout my childhood. Although I had little awareness of what marriage would mean, I could not possibly back out; arrangements had gone too far.

Doris, my foster mother, wanted to organise things her way. It was an opportunity to show off in the village church to all her family and friends, which was ironic since she had always been quick to declare, "She's not ours, of course."

My fiancé's family didn't want anything so grand. My future sister-in-law, who was good at dressmaking, kindly offered to make my dress and those of my three bridesmaids. Doris was furious about this and threatened to have no more to do with me. I managed to soothe her and plans were put in place eventually. My wedding dress was just as elegant as I hoped.

On the morning of the wedding I was nervous. My stick-on nails began to peel off, and I could not get the hang of the veil. When I was dressed finally, I left my bedroom and met Doris on the stairs. She had taken no interest in my dress at all.

"How do I look?" I asked.

"You'll do," was her terse reply.

She began to harangue me because Tom was not yet back from his paper rounds. I had a sick feeling in my stomach, as I knew she was going to ruin my day; to her, it was not *my* day at all. The service was to be at 2pm. Tom arrived back at 1.40pm. I made sandwiches for him whilst he slowly shaved, washed and changed into his suit. He said not a word, and I anxiously wondered how he really felt about giving me away. I was at screaming point when Doris tripped off to the church without an encouraging word to either Tom or me. We set out at 2.15pm. There were some humorous comments from guests after the service about us arriving late when we lived just across the road from the church. I guess most who knew Tom understood why.

The day passed in a haze. I felt as if it was not happening to me. We left for a honeymoon in Cornwall and a new life.

———

We moved into a small cottage in the village of Holbrook and soon made many friends. Every evening, my husband liked to go to the pub just opposite our cottage. I should have seen the warning signs, but I decided to go along with his chosen lifestyle. I started work back at the old library building again, alongside one of my college friends. The lack of resources and the restrictions of the building were frustrating to us. We had been excited at college with the new ideas we had for the education of these children, but the reality was that there were no suitable buildings or resources to do much more than frustrating childminding. I used to scour junk shops at weekends to buy suitable equipment to work with the children. I remember struggling to get onto the bus one morning, carrying a baby bath and a bag of sand to create a sand play area for little ones. The bus driver always had a humorous comment to make.

CHAPTER FOURTEEN

Mums and Dads

I HAD THE CONFUSION IN MY GROWING-UP YEARS OF BEING required to call a number of people Mum or Dad after I had lost contact with my own parents. My foster parents encouraged me to use these labels, though they did not in the end adopt me and claim me as their child. In married life, I called my in-laws Mum or Dad (as appropriate). Having been married three times, that's a lot of surrogate parents. In their different ways, they were all lovely and loving people, and I saw examples of good, close family relationships from them. I was always included and cared about, even though my life must have seemed strange to them. The reaction I had from both of my first two husbands to my story was that they told me to put it all behind me, forget it, and just live in the here and now. During the busy years of my career and motherhood, that was fairly easy to achieve.

⸺◦⸺

Becoming a mother for the first time was exciting but very scary. I had had one miscarriage before my first son was born, and so he was a very-much-wanted baby. I had no real role models to help me know what my role should be. I had no one to lean on for support and advice; Dr Spock's book was my bible. I wanted children very much and knew I would be a loving mum. I had enough experience of working with children to know that life would be very different in future. Because of my work I was acutely aware of how things can go wrong in pregnancy, so it was an anxious time for me.

This pregnancy went well, apart from my craving to eat coal, which became a secret habit whenever I could get hold of a lump.

Like most first-time parents, I never realised how hard it would be to bring up a baby and make a good job of it. This was a difficult time for me, too, having no family to help me. It was one of the few times in my life when I wished that I had a mum to lean on.

Shaun was born on a snowy day in January 1968, in a rural cottage-maternity hospital, where each mum stayed for ten days to recover from her labour. Shaun's was a difficult birth, which resulted in lots of stitches for me. I sat on a blow-up swimming ring for months, which caused much hilarity. Each newborn baby was whisked away at night, and each mother was expected to get a good night's sleep. Oh, it was bliss! Nowadays, mothers usually stay in hospital for just a few hours, and get no time to recover before going home and beginning the rounds of feeding, etc. and suffering from broken sleep.

When I first saw my son, I was overwhelmed by emotions of love and protectiveness. He was very small, with a head of long, auburn-coloured hair. We joked about it, but later it made sense because my sister also produced children with red hair. I now know my dad was called 'Red' because of his red hair colour.

On the morning after he was born, Shaun, with the other babies, was delivered to our small ward swaddled in a tight cotton sheet, ready for feeding and yelling at the top of his voice. He developed jaundice at a few days old – he was identified as a 'rhesus baby' – and he needed to be transferred to the Children's Hospital in Derby. My first caring for him was alone in the mother-and-baby unit at the children's hospital, where he was put under an ultraviolet (UV) lamp for several hours a day.

He showed his personality early in life; he was lively, restless and needed little sleep. Before he was two years old, he found a way to climb out of his cot by piling the covers up at one end. He had a baby walker and soon discovered the way to unlock the safety door out of the kitchen. Unfortunately, beyond this door was a flight of stone steps, and I heard the bump, bump, bump as he went head over heels down them. No damage was done, thankfully.

Shaun, at two, was very dependent on his dummy, and would tear around in his little car with one hanging out of his mouth, like a fag, whilst he chatted. He found a way to throw them out of the window – we lived in a first-floor flat at the time. I warned him one day that if he did it again, I would throw all the dummies in the bin. He did; I did; and, much to my amazement, he never wanted one again. Our little grandson, William, was reluctant to give up his dummy. I told him the story about his uncle, Shaun. He listened with a smile, declared he didn't want his dummy anymore, asked to put it in the bin, then popped it back in his mouth. Thankfully, the day soon arrived when his mum persuaded him to give his dummy to the 'dee dee fairy', who left a new fire-engine toy in its place, and the dummy was forgotten.

Shaun has always had a great personality. I am immensely proud of all that he has achieved in his life – he makes me laugh and sometimes amazes me too – but he is a loving, thoughtful, entertaining son. He gets on well with all sorts of people and has worked his way up to the successful job he now has. He's kind and forgiving, and he has his father's sense of humour with an adventurous spirit. He has been headhunted for jobs three times in his life and his present employer appears to value him. He loves outdoor activities, and is mad about scuba diving, cars, skiing, travel and golf. Sadly, he never met his father again after the age of two; history was repeated. We separated when we lost our home, and I took on the full-time care of our son and returned to teaching. At the time of writing this book, Shaun is engaged to his partner, Jannette, who has brought our precious grandson Dylan into our lives and a sense of loving stability to Shaun's life. Shaun and Dylan are very close, and, finally, Shaun has achieved his wish to teach Dylan to scuba dive, which they now share a love for.

I am enormously proud of both my sons. They have achieved more than I could ever have dreamed of and have each come through lots of adversity. They are kind, loving people and excellent parents, and they think the world of me, despite my many mistakes. They have each produced wonderful grandchildren, and are always glad to include John and me in their lives.

For some months after the birth, I struggled with post-natal depression. I had a baby who was active and demanding from the start, and who slept badly. I was reduced to tears easily and felt very inadequate as a mum. I was given tablets by my doctor to relieve my anxieties, which gave me weird side effects – the patterns on the carpet began to move around as I tried to focus. Eventually, I was referred to a psychiatrist, who only asked about my moods and changed my medications; post-natal depression was not recognised and I just had to carry on as best I could.

As a result of these problems, I found breastfeeding difficult and had to stop. Early motherhood was fraught with fears and loneliness. I found one good friend in the village, a young mother who was just recovering from similar mental illness, and she was a source of great comfort to me. In the end, my symptoms died away, but it was a long time before I began to feel confident as a mum and happy again.

Managing a hardware shop was a step too far and led to our financial bankruptcy. My fears about the marriage had been realised, and we separated in September 1969. Throughout this time, my husband's sister had been a great support, but she lived a few miles away, and, with having no car and managing the shop, I was not able to see much of her. A friend helped me find a room in a house owned by an elderly widower in a small mining town.

I was offered employment straight away, at the brand-new, purpose-built special school that had replaced the old library building. I was grateful for the opportunity to earn and keep my baby with me. I spent a term at the school. It was extremely hard going, as I had to leave at 7am to take my infant son by bus to a childminder and then catch another bus to school, but it did get me back into the work that I loved and could do well, and it rebuilt my confidence gradually. However, one more incident during this time nearly felled me.

The old gentleman I was renting a room from seemed kind at first, and let me use the kitchen and bathroom freely. Shaun slept in his cot in my small bedroom. One night, as I was drifting off to sleep, the door opened slowly and the 'nice' old gentleman crept in and tried to get into my bed. A furious tussle ensued, I got him out by threatening to alert the neighbours, and the next morning I said I was leaving. He put all my belongings on the street whilst I was at work and friends took me in. I had experienced enough of the bad side of predatory men to make me wary and very independent. Like other women in this situation, I felt guilty for putting myself at risk once more. But I didn't know anyone who'd had a similar experience, so I didn't tell anyone. I felt I would be blamed for all that had happened in recent months. Once again, I could not comprehend how an old, ugly man could do this to me. I still had a lot to learn.

CHAPTER FIFTEEN

Going Solo

In January 1970, just as I was despairing of being able to cope, I was interviewed for a new job – a new, small day centre was opening in Ashbourne, where I had been to school. This would allow me to begin a new phase in my life, alone with my young son, Shaun. I found a small flat in the town's market square, and a warm, friendly woman to care for my infant son as I started a new job.

Our rented flat in the town was above a toy shop. At weekends, Shaun used to spend a lot of time gazing in the window, and telling me and the staff which toys he wanted. They were kind and would put a toy aside for me whilst I saved up for it; Shaun nagged me each weekend to go and get it.

It was a happy time for us both, though it was difficult to manage everything alone, but – with the help of the childminder and my work – we managed. I marvel now at how little paperwork there was in those days in my role as head of the day centre and how all my school holidays were free for me to be with my son.

⁂

Shaun's father, who objected to my move to Ashbourne, visited us a few times, but never regularly. He was most reluctant to help me financially. Eventually, I said he must either see his son and support him on a secure basis or stay away. We never saw him again; he found it too difficult to believe that I did not love him anymore, nor did I trust him to look after us. It was all very sad. We were divorced in 1972, and my lovely boy was never able to meet his father from then on – it was like history repeating itself. As Shaun has grown up he reminds me a lot of his dad – he has the same happy-go-lucky personality, is hard-working, is very focussed on his goals and has a great sense of humour. He has made a successful career for himself and has been headhunted three times in his career by new companies.

I had lost touch with my foster parents some years before my return to Ashbourne, but I saw Doris just once in the town after I moved there. She had somehow heard about my situation. She had left Tom by that time and had moved to another village with a man called Bill. When Tom heard about this, he simply said, "Poor Bill!"

One day, during my first month back in the town, she saw me standing with Shaun outside our favourite toy shop and came over to me with a face like thunder. She began to harangue me about what a stupid girl I had been and how she always knew I would end up like this. She did not look at my son or acknowledge him in any way, which hurt a lot. For the first and only time I stood up to her and said, "You obviously don't care about me. You've never cared. We don't need you. Goodbye."

I never spoke to her again. I realised I had an unforgiving nature, as a result of all the rejection I had experienced. Now, in carrying out research for my book, I understand the bigger picture.

It was a time of unhappy endings and exciting new beginnings. I often felt lonely and fearful of the future, yet I was supported by the new people working with me and new friends. I was acutely aware that my presence back in the town where I had been at school would be known, and I worried what my old teachers and school friends would say. A mother alone with a toddler was still a cause for criticism in those days. However, I experienced much kindness and understanding from my old teachers whom I met in the town. I expected criticism and rejection, but found that people were complimentary about how I coped with all that was happening to me. It still didn't dawn on me that they all knew the score and cared about me.

The town of Ashbourne and its surrounding villages had no provision for disabled children at that time. I was appointed to open a small day centre for eight children in an old building, which had been a Territorial Army base during the Second World War. It was only a small step up from working in old church halls and a disused library.

This was my first experience of starting something from scratch, being in charge, interviewing staff, purchasing suitable equipment and organising a structure for the children's activities. I was called a teaching supervisor, and had three assistants initially and a dinner lady.

Children of all ages up to sixteen were brought to and from the Cokayne Centre, as it was called, by taxis and minibuses each day. Meals were provided from a local school, and we had a tiny yard for the children to play outside. None of this was ideal, but we managed.

Opposite the building was the town's spacious park, with a kiddies' playground. We would take the children there each day, weather permitting, for some exercise and ball games.

I had some lovely women working with me, and there was a lot of fun and mutual support. They were patient with me, since I was younger than most of them and had a lot to learn. None of them had any previous experience of these children, so I was slightly ahead of them. The lessons I had gleaned from my college training stood me in good stead. I was determined to enable the children to gain as many experiences of everyday activities as we could.

Shopping in the town, just a short walk away, was the first venture. Most of the children had never been taken to a shop and had no experience of being amongst ordinary people whom they did not know. With such small numbers, we could give each of them an individual experience. They had to be taught the many social skills that the rest of us take for granted. Gradually, I persuaded their mothers to send a small shopping list to us, and their child was able to buy these items, often by recognising the packets or jars they had at home. They handled real money and change, and took these items home proudly at the end of the day. Initially, we were met with a mixed response from some people in the town, who would say in a loud voice, "Those children should not be allowed out."

Needless to say, we explained carefully what we were about, and people could see that the children were well behaved generally, and taught to say please and thank you. The children gained hugely in confidence, and the townsfolk began slowly to recognise and acknowledge them with friendly greetings. There were occasional problems. We ventured into the new Co-op self-service shop. The children soon put everything and anything in the trolley, and it was mayhem. I was given a box of chocolates for them quietly and asked to, "Take them away."

On another shopping trip, I exited a bookshop and walked up the street with 'Susie' who said, "Do you like the book I got for you?"

To my horror, I discovered she had taken a book off a shelf and put it in my shopping bag. This was not the last time I had to return, red-faced and explain our 'theft'.

I came up with the idea of approaching the headteacher of a nearby junior school to see if we could use their gym hall for our children to have some exercise. He was enthusiastic and got agreement from his staff for our little group to join one class a week. I was simply looking for somewhere for the children to mix with others and have a bit of exercise.

In 1970, the idea of integrating severely disabled children from our day centre with junior school children was unheard of. I had to explain to the education authorities why such a move would be beneficial to all those involved. The junior school had to get agreement from their children's parents, some of whom queried whether their child would 'catch anything' from being in contact with disabled children. I persevered and, eventually, we established a weekly gym session with little opposition. The children looked forward to this activity each week.

Similarly, they joined a group at a local swimming pool and became individual members of the local library. I had regular visits from the council adviser who was tasked with monitoring my strange activities, as he saw them!

For our first Christmas, we decided to put on a pantomime for the local population. Staff and pupils all had a part to play, and we had an audience of parents and the local press, whom I think had grown used to the unusual events at the day centre by this time. Parents began to notice the increased independence of their children and their improving communication skills.

In 1971, I became a probationary teacher. It happened this way. Mencap, the national group for parents of mentally handicapped children, had lobbied Parliament for some years to have the term 'excluded from education' removed from their children's medical notes. When Parliament successfully passed a bill to effectively allow all children – whatever their circumstances – to attend mainstream schools, it was to have far-reaching implications and consequences, which could not have been foreseen at the time: the possibility that these children would be going to a local school just like every other child. That was a long way off then. There were many barriers to break down in the teaching professions and with society in general. Eventually, an Act of Parliament achieved this goal, and our little day centre became a school, along with all other such establishments in the country.

It was decided by the then Department for Education and Science that staff such as I, who had trained for two years, could only be given the status of 'teacher' after a further probationary period of five years. This meant that, although I had been working in this occupation for six years, I would have to wait another five years to be recognised fully as a qualified teacher. In addition, after that time, I and others like me could apply to teach in any type of school or study for a degree in education. There were moves to provide additional training for us, and I was lucky enough to be sent to a teacher-training college for one year, where the syllabus was all about the assessment of children's development and the teaching of reading, which I found very useful. Ultimately, the training of teachers of children with special needs became a three-year university course at graduate level.

CHAPTER SIXTEEN

A Bobby, Bombs and a Bingo Hall

BY THE THIRD YEAR AT THE LITTLE SCHOOL, NUMBERS HAD grown considerably. The local education department had agreed to a request from the school governors to enlarge our old two-storey building by adding a temporary classroom at the back. The day came when a digger arrived, much to the children's excitement. The driver set to and began to dig. The noise was horrendous, and the children were high as kites as they had never seen a digger working before. After a short time, the noise stopped, the driver came into the building and showed me the dirty, rusty, metal object that he had unearthed.

"I don't want to worry you, but this looks like a hand grenade to me," he said. "What do you want me to do with it?"

As I was digesting this information he left the 'grenade' on my desk and went back to his work. What was I to do? I knew the building had been used as a base for the Territorial Army during the Second World War, but I did not know that the practice at the end of the war was to dig a big hole and bury all surplus ammunition. I rang the local police, who were incredulous and did not believe that the object could be a grenade, but said they would send a bobby round.

About half an hour later, just as the digger driver appeared with two more muddy bits of metal, a police constable arrived. He took a long look, huffed and puffed a bit and said, "Have you got a bucket?"

I fetched a bucket and, at his request, filled it with water. He popped the 'grenades' into it, put the bucket into his car boot and drove away. The digger driver, quite sensibly, refused to continue working, but informed me somewhat grumpily that he was on a contract and had to be finished by tomorrow.

I thought it was time to ring the education office for advice. It was always a tricky venture to get anyone to give advice over the phone and even more difficult to actually speak to a senior officer, since I was a lowly minion in a very large organisation. However, I plucked up the courage.

"Hello, can I speak to the assistant education officer?" I asked.

"What is it concerning?" queried the person who had answered the phone.

"Well, a bomb, actually; it was under our playground. There appear to be several more. A man with a JCB is digging them up, and the police have advised us we have to evacuate the building, now. I need some advice."

"*Who* are you?"

I explained once more.

"Just a moment."

Five minutes later, the person returned to the phone and asked, "Where are you speaking from? Are you sure this is true?"

And on and on it went whilst I hung on in the red public phone box, rapidly feeding pennies into the slot, since I was not allowed back into the school building. Eventually, I was told to hold on whilst the big chief, the assistant director, came to the phone. After further questioning – with a hint of sarcasm and disbelief, he decided to contact the army, belatedly accepting that we were in an old Territorial Army depot and we had an urgent problem.

The rest of the day was a nightmare of trying to contact parents, not all of whom had a phone, sending messages to taxi companies to get the children home and to our escort ladies who accompanied the children in the taxis, and keeping calm. The army arrived in numbers, with a dapper senior officer who wasted no time in closing the whole site and the street, excluding us from the building permanently. Children and staff were left standing on the roadside like orphans.

A couple of days later, a considerable pile of old ammunition that had been buried at the end of the war was carefully removed from the site, watched over by army personnel – no one was allowed near the street to watch. The ammunition was taken to a rural location for a controlled explosion. I was told that we would not be able to return to the site for a couple of weeks, until all the ground had been turned over and the army could be satisfied that it was safe. This took eight weeks because of the tricky decisions to be made about who should pay for the work.

I was in touch with the education office constantly – ringing, at my own expense, from the public call box outside my flat. I was asked by the assistant director if I knew of any other site in the town where the children could be taught meanwhile. I didn't think this was part of my job description, but tried to be helpful. The only free building we could find was next to the busy bus station, in an ex-cinema building that had been turned into a bingo club and dance hall.

The education officer and I went to view the building. It had a large dance/bingo hall, which was a plus in terms of space, but had multiple exits, a bar, and deliveries of beer barrels, food and stores of all kinds during the daytime; it was hardly suitable for the children in our care. He agreed reluctantly that it would have to do, and arrangements were made for us to move in.

⸎

The children took it all in their stride. Some tried several times to dash out and board a bus at the nearby bus station. Most days, managing escaping children took on a new urgency. We were in that building for four months, including the time taken to put the extra classroom in place. I remember that time as one of continuous laughter and fun. The children rose to the occasion and would give us daily performances on the stage with a pretend microphone.

There was a lovely teenage boy, Paddy, who was confined to a wheelchair, with no use of his lower limbs. He could communicate only with squeaks, nudges and pointing. If he happened to be having his nappy changed just as the brewery delivery man trundled by with crates and barrels of beer, exclaiming nonchalantly, "Don't mind me," Paddy would protest with a loud squeak, point to the man and then to his nappy area, and shake his head vigorously, sending us into fits of giggles. He knew everything that went on in the place and would alert us by his variety of sounds if any other child was misbehaving. We all loved him dearly.

To pass the time, there were a lot of singing games and dancing to amuse the children, for whom any semblance of proper lessons was hopeless. The children accepted all the changes as part of everyday normality – they were brilliant.

In the end, we moved back into our school, which by then had a brand-new portable building attached by a corridor to the old brick one, and a brand-new play area, which made up for all the hassle we had gone through. I had my own office and had a typewriter for the first time, together with a place to talk to visitors in private. My door was usually left open and children would wander in, perch at my desk and pretend to answer the phone. It was such a happy time.

In 1972, I was married for the second time, and we moved into a semi-detached house just outside the town centre, with a mortgage of £8,500, which seemed an enormous amount at that time. The house, which had been built in the 1940s, had a large garden with an orchard, which was ideal for children to play in. We always had children coming to play with Shaun when he was young. It was a happy time for all of us. My new husband, Patrick, agreed to adopt Shaun as his son since we had lost all contact with his father. Shaun has said that he had a happy childhood. When we had our first car, we went out into the countryside a lot and enjoyed walking with our Labrador.

I was busy with my teaching career, and it was another eight years before David arrived. I was then, at thirty-four, classed as an older mother by the doctors. David had dark hair, and was a quiet, contented baby. I was again bowled over by the love I felt and the need to care for him, always. Nowadays, skin contact is recognised as an important way for mothers and fathers to bond with their babies. I remember talking to him softly that first night, and promising him that I would always love and care for him and wondering what he would make of his life. I could not imagine that he would grow up to be the first in our family to go to university, to get a first-class degree and, subsequently, to be awarded a doctorate.

David is extremely modest and self-effacing, and very loving. He has a gentle but positive way with his sons, and is involved in their development in ways that were undreamed of when I was first a parent: changing nappies, wiping bottoms and never seeming to mind when they prevent him from his love of watching sport. They all share a love of being out in the countryside.

He is married to Alison, a teacher, who is a brilliant mum, and fills her sons' lives with songs and entertainment. Alison says Dave is the number one person to his sons, William and Nathaniel. They are such a happy family.

CHAPTER SEVENTEEN

Much-loved Grandparents

GEORGE AND CONNIE WERE MY SECOND HUSBAND'S parents. They lived on the edge of the town and ran a greengrocery shop. They accepted me into their family readily.

Connie was an interesting and affectionate grandmother. She was always ready with a story or a tease for each of her grandchildren, and treated them all the same, including my son Shaun. She had a lively personality, a lovely smile and always made us feel welcome. She worked hard all her life and brought up three children whilst her husband was involved in the Second World War. She lived on for several years after his death then sadly died of a stroke.

We had some wonderful times with them at Christmas when they were both still alive and active. It was a time to get all the family together at their house or the houses of their children. The little ones always wanted a game of charades and, for some unexplained reason, whatever the charade, granddad had to be a bear with a fur hat on. They would always say, "Granddad's in my team," and he had to wear the hat, no matter how vague a connection. They wanted him to be involved. The resulting playacting left us all crying with laughter.

On a number of occasions, the party would be at our house, and I, being a teacher, was expected to organise the children to put on a play and then play games. Usually, having been through several parties in my school and starting my holiday absolutely tired out, this was a tall order. However, we had a lot of fun. They loved a game called Murder in the Dark, and would order one of the adults to go and hide whilst they counted to a hundred – and argued about when they got there, often starting their counting again, with the girls being the most argumentative. Eventually, they would run around the house trying to find the victim. Once, my husband lay in the bath and covered himself with a white towel. As a child walked in, he rose up with a groan, and the little one ran shrieking and crying downstairs. I miss those family times and I myself learned a lot about being a good grandma.

George was a lovely man and a perfect granddad. During the summer holidays in 1980, he was seriously ill with cancer. As I waited for the delivery day of our second baby, and whilst he was still able to get about, he would walk across the town to our house every day to take our Labrador for a walk on the Tissington Trail, which runs through a local area of natural beauty. We had a cuppa on his return and talked about everything except his illness. Cancer was seldom referred to in those days. George was close to death as our son David arrived in September. George was being nursed at home by his wife and daughter, and we were anxious for him to see his latest grandchild. Our first call after leaving the hospital with our son was to see his granddad George, who was weak, but able to talk.

I said, "Look who we've brought to meet you, Dad."

"Let's have a look at him," George declared.

We put the baby in the crook of his arm, because he was too weak to hold him.

He looked longingly at the little one. "Look after him for me, won't you?" was all he said.

We promised to do that and to tell David about his granddad when he was older. I have kept that promise, and both David and Shaun have a love of stories about him.

A few days later he died. He was a truly lovely man, and I loved him dearly.

CHAPTER EIGHTEEN

"I Am Your Mother"

MY SISTER HAD ASKED ME ONCE IF I HAD ANY INFORMATION that could help us find our birth parents. I remembered that I had a copy of my birth certificate, on which was the address where I was born, at a house on Streatham Hill, in South East London. We looked at the document, and she copied the address. I heard no more about this until, in February 1970, a photograph arrived with a letter from my mother.

It began, "Hello, Anita, this is your mum writing to you."

The letter said that the photo showed my mother on holiday with her husband and her sister.

"That's me in the middle" she wrote.

I was stunned. I felt bewildered by the casualness of her letter. I was twenty-five, and I had not seen her since I was three. I had never expected to find her.

I did not recognise her nor her sister, though I now know I had spent time with them when I was a toddler. I contacted my sister and she told me that her husband had been working in London and had found the house where I was born. A man came to the door; he was my mother's brother and he said that my mother was living in Camberwell Green. They took my brother-in-law round to meet my mum and Jim, her second husband, and they had a long chat.

Me 'playing out'

Fred Venes, my dad

Peggy Payne, my mum

My maternal grandparents, Thomas Mccallum
and his wife May Ellen

Three sisters – Sandra, Elaine, Anita

My brother, Graham, as Potts, the clown

My dad's second family – Peter, Elaine and Tony

Meeting Graham for the first time

My eldest son, Shaun and his family, Jannette and Dylan

David, my second son, and his family, Alison, William and Natty

Cello practice

Another hobby

Shaun and me with Dave at his graduation

Mum and Jim at our home

Dave's wedding day

John and me on our wedding day

When I had got over the shock of hearing from my mother, I wrote to her, telling her about my current life. In due course, I decided to go down to London to meet her.

I was filled with mixed emotions as we travelled by train to St Pancras and took the Tube to Elephant and Castle, where my mum and her husband Jim would be waiting. We missed each other, and I had to take a taxi to their flat. They were standing at the roadside looking anxiously at each taxi as I got out, hoisted out my heavy pushchair and bags, and turned to meet her.

She greeted me with a peck on the cheek and said, "Hello, dear."

Just that, after over twenty years apart.

I didn't know how to feel. I wanted to hear that she loved me and had missed me for all those years when we had been apart. I wanted a hug. I wanted to tell her how unhappy I had been growing up without her love. I didn't feel able to start any of those conversations. The happy reunion I had hoped for did not happen. I spent my time with them in a daze, feeling it was all unreal. I wanted to ask her how she felt about seeing me again.

The atmosphere was tense and uneasy. Conversation over the weekend was stilted and strained, and it was clear that she did not want to discuss anything about the past. Jim was quick to butt in to say she did not need to 'rake up the past'. They seemed to have no idea about how much my sister and I would want to know about our history, not least why we were put into care at such a young age. My son Shaun, then aged two and lively, was a puzzle to them. They had no idea how to behave with an active infant. There was no feeling of a grandmother meeting her grandson for the first time and no cuddles. I realised finally that my mother had no knowledge of how unhappy my time with foster parents had been. Sadly, I had to come to terms with the reality that our relationship could never be a close one, and I was no nearer to finding out why we had been placed in care as babies.

When I returned home, I was asked how it went and my sad response was greeted with disbelief.

When I remarried in 1972, my mum did not come to my wedding, and I was not surprised by her lack of interest. However, I kept in touch by phone and, when we had settled into our new home, she and her husband travelled to stay with us in Ashbourne several times over the next few years.

Mum often seemed ill at ease. There was no emotional connection between us nor with her husband, as far as I could tell. She would sit and stare into space for long periods, and had no enthusiasm for deciding what to do. She had severe asthma, yet she smoked constantly and ate little. I did not know then how ill she was. She was bewildered by the open countryside all around us when we took her out in the car and she wondered how we could ever find our way about. I told her that was how we felt travelling around in London. She spoke of enjoying her stay and, although a year or more would pass before she could be persuaded to visit us again, she seemed pleased to do so. It was always difficult, and left me feeling exhausted and sad after trying to create a family atmosphere.

One summer when it was Mum and Jim's fortieth wedding anniversary, we invited them to stay with us. We organised a meal out in the countryside at a lovely restaurant, and my sister and her partner joined us for a celebratory lunch. It was a beautiful June day and, after lunch, we sat in our garden, chatting.

Out of the blue, Mum said to me suddenly, "I saw you in London once, when you were fifteen."

My sister and I looked at each other in amazement.

My mum went on, "The Children's Society wrote to me to ask me if I would like to see you and perhaps have you back. We couldn't decide what to do, but Jim said why not go along and see how you feel. So we went to their head office. We waited in a corridor and you walked straight past us."

The hairs on the back of my neck stood on end and I felt very strange. I had been to London just once in my teens. Immediately, my mind jumped back to that long-ago day when I was taken by a social worker to The Children's Society head office on my way to stay with my penfriend in France.

"What happened?" I asked.

"Well, we couldn't make our minds up," Mum explained. "Jim said he would support me if I decided to have you back. I knew that Sandra had been adopted. I was nervous about going there. They said we could wait and see how I felt when I saw you. I didn't know what to expect. When you came past me, you looked so happy and well that I didn't think I could take you away from your home and unsettle you, so we kept quiet. I said no, I couldn't take you back, and that was that. I didn't know you were not happy in the foster home. I didn't know if I would ever see you again. It made me very sad."

That phrase "I couldn't take you back" hurt a lot – it was as if I had been banished like a naughty child and was not deserving of another chance of being with my mother. She must have been told that I was unhappy with my foster parents. I can't imagine what my reaction might have been at that time, if she had spoken to me in that bleak corridor, when I knew nothing about her. Nor what my decision might have been if she had wanted me back with her. My whole future would have been different. By that time, my sister had been adopted and living in Cumbria, and so there was no possibility that Mum would consider having us both back with her.

Many more years passed before I learned that Mum had serious mental health problems and could not have looked after us when we were small. At fifteen, I would have resented being moved away from the rural countryside that I loved and from all my school friends too. I now believe that Mum's mental condition stemmed from the trauma of losing contact with her children and that her decision on that day in London was a wise one for both of us. But I could not understand how she could have seen me and not wanted to speak to me.

After that visit to our home, I put this behind me, kept in regular contact with her and vowed never to give up my children, no matter what happened. I have been very successful at putting bad memories out of my mind. Knowing how strong my love is for both my sons, I can understand some of the pain she went through.

———∞———

During the welfare officer's visit in 1987, she suggested that I might try to get my mother to talk about the past. We all arrive in this world with a mother. Losing your mother for whatever reason is a huge trauma when you are a small child, and particularly so if no one explains why, and all memories of her are forgotten or buried.

So, taking up this idea, I wrote to Mum. I told her that I had discovered information about my brother and said I felt sorry for her that she had had to give him up as well as us. I told her I would like to know something about my father. I also told her I loved her and held no grudge for all that had happened to me.

My mother later wrote the following letter to me, explaining for the first time some of the background to her history:

I did not know that you were consulting a psychiatrist and I am glad that it has helped you, I don't agree with dragging up the past, although I feel it might help you with your problems. It is something I try to block out of my conscience, this I have tried to do for so many years, but as you know right up to these days I still have to have some sort of treatment and that is only because in the back of my mind there was the guilt. I am not going to excuse myself for the past but I do know that [it is] owing to having a father who was a drunk, and a mother who had so many children before I came along [that] she couldn't cope and left me. So it must have been history repeating itself. You say, Anita, that you love me very much, I only wish that I could feel worthy of this but I can't, and I too feel a barrier between us when we meet, but I want you to know that both Jim and I are always here if ever you need someone to chat to and I am sure you would find that Jim is very understanding and helpful, as it was only by him being so understanding and patient with me that I am like I am today, for he has a lot to put up with over the years. As for your brother, Graham, I had not mentioned him to Jim and I do hope for everyone concerned that things can be left as they are, but I must just trust in your own judgement. And now I must say you must stop saying sorry to me for I feel that you might end up feeling guilty about me. You have nothing to reproach yourself for as you have certainly proved what a caring person you are by doing the work you have done all these years. So, Anita, I will close now[,] hoping that you find what you are looking for very soon. All our love Mum

This was the closest we ever came to a frank declaration of our feelings. A further letter came just nine days later:

Since I wrote to you last week I have been doing a lot of thinking about you and I have read and re-read your letter several times over, and I realise that you do need some one [sic] to care for you[,] for you seem to have had your share of let downs and heartaches, and if I can be any comfort to you then I am willing to try to earn your love and respect. After reading your letter again it certainly made me very happy to know that you had forgiven me. I only wish we lived nearer but at least we can keep in touch by phone. I do envy folks when they talk about going places and doing things with their families.

… before I close I must tell you that Graham was not the child of your father. It was someone I thought wanted me, but as soon as I became pregnant he hopped off, hence he (Graham)

went to foster parents as soon as I came out of hospital, pending adoption, he was then two weeks old, so you [can] see why, as long as I live, in the back in my mind I still feel unworthy as regards to children. I was very lucky to meet Jim, you may find this rather strange [but] there wasn't any love between us when we first got married, Jim felt sorry for me as I went back home to my parents and was more than welcome because to them it was a bit more money coming into the house [which was] mostly spent on drink, and after a few months Jim asked me if I would like to marry him to get me out of a bad situation, he was really like a good Samaritan and I must say that as one gets older you become very close. I really do not know what I would do if I am left without him…

P.S. I hope I haven't offended you in any way, love Mum

Her humble words affected me a lot. They were the most loving words that ever passed between us, but were never referred to again. I never felt able to burden her with my worries.

These letters came at a time of great turmoil for me. I saw clearly the lifelong effect on her of the separation from her children, because I was a mother myself by this time. I could feel some of the anguish she must have gone through. Declaring my forgiveness, even in a letter, was very helpful to me. Once, in conversation, she said my father was no good and I was better off not knowing about him. These issues were never ever raised with her again. I have often regretted not pursuing my childhood history with her, but, as I became aware of her fragile state of mind, I did not want to add to her anxieties. Jim always stood between us to protect Mum.

We never spent Christmas together, although they did come to our house for short holidays on many occasions. Once, when I visited them in London, they took me to meet my mother's sister, Eileen. She was the only other relative of my mother that I ever saw.

CHAPTER NINETEEN

Life and Death

MY FIRST HUSBAND'S PARENTS, STAN AND ALICE, LIVED IN a terraced house in Derby. They were a devoted couple. When I met them, they were near to retiring age – Stan still worked part-time for the town's parks department and had a love of gardening. We would often find him at his allotment, where he grew many kinds of vegetables, and he was keen for us to sample anything that was ready to eat. They were both very kind to me; they were always puzzled about my background and concerned because I was eight years younger than their son. It was the time of short skirts and high heels, and they did not always approve of my outfits.

I knew my first husband's parents for a relatively short time. One day, in the autumn of 1967, Stan was brought home from his work due to feeling unwell. A doctor was sent for and, after he had arrived and examined Stan, he declared that he thought Stan was having a heart attack and called an ambulance. Alice flopped down into a chair, exclaimed, "Oh no!" and died immediately of a massive heart attack. This was a terrible tragedy for all of us. Stan had to stay in hospital for weeks and missed her funeral. I was pregnant with Shaun, and so his grandmother never got to see him. Stan lived on for many more years in the home of his daughter, son-in-law and their children, and was able to enjoy knowing his grandson Shaun. Heart disease was prevalent in both families, and my husband later died of a heart attack in his early forties.

—⊶⊷—

The telephone rang at home one day in 1984, and I answered it.

"Hello, is that Anita?" asked the caller. "This is Dawn speaking; do you know where my mother is?"

I did not need to ask who it was; I knew instinctively that this was the Dawn who had been my sister's beautiful baby all those years ago. We chatted for a while, and she told me that she had only heard the whole story from her adoptive parents/grandparents recently, and wanted to find her birth mother.

I told her, "Yes, I do know where she is and I have her phone number. I think I had better ring her first before I give you her number."

I ended the conversation with Dawn and I rang Sandra immediately.

"Sandra, I have some news for you. Are you sitting down?" I asked her.

"Why? What's happened?" queried Sandra.

"I've just had a call from Dawn. She wants to speak to you."

There was a long pause and then she replied, "Oh, that's a surprise. What shall I do?"

We talked, and she was persuaded to ring Dawn, which she did.

Then began a long and mostly happy relationship for them both, which I have been pleased to support. Strangely, if they had not met I would never have found the rest of my family in the years ahead. Dawn is a lovely, lively, entertaining image of her mum, and we have had some great times together.

CHAPTER TWENTY

A Sad Ending

AFTER OUR FIRST MEETING, I KEPT IN TOUCH WITH MY mum from time to time. There would be long gaps when I did not hear from her, and, ultimately, when she wrote or answered the phone, she would say vaguely that she had not been well. It was another decade before I persuaded her husband to tell me why she was in hospital again.

"*Schizophrenia*," was his shocking reply. "She's had it for years; ever since I've known her," said Jim.

I was extremely alarmed; I was sad for her and him, and scared for my children and me. I was ignorant about the disease.

He told me that she had spent many periods in a mental hospital, just up the road from where they lived. I did not know how to react to this news. He said that on no account could I visit her in hospital, as she did not want my sister and me to see her there, or to know about her illness; she was ashamed.

Some years, she was well enough for both of them to travel to our house by coach from London. She would enjoy trips around the countryside and visits to local pubs. She always had a distant, sad look about her. She chain-smoked all the time, and became quite thin and drawn in her face. Her husband was always fiercely protective of her, and it made it difficult for her and me to spend time together without him speaking up for her. It was good that she had his strong support, since most of their relatives shunned her and did not visit them.

In later years, when she spent increasing amounts of time in the Maudsley Hospital, we would often travel down to see her there – we found it was better not to forewarn her. The locked ward was oppressive. Every patient smoked, and the atmosphere was chaotic, threatening, and unhelpful to patients and visitors. Mum stayed in her room most of the time. We discovered that she was able to get permission to leave the ward because she had not been sectioned.

One day, wearing her nightwear, she wandered out of the ward and the hospital grounds, and made her way home, some distance away. Finding her husband was not at home, she went to the hairdressers for a cut and blow dry. No one had noticed her leaving the hospital. She told the hairdresser cheerfully that she thought she had an appointment.

Jim was regaling her constantly in front of us about how she begged him to take something into the hospital – a tea service, jewellery or money – which she promptly gave away.

Her confusion grew worse with age. I only once experienced her hearing 'voices', when she told me the Russians were outside waiting to get her. My tactic was to tell her not to worry about it, but Jim had to argue about it and tensions grew until one day when she bashed him with her handbag and would not come out of her room when he visited. She told me she wanted a divorce, and to come and live with us. All this was heartbreaking because she was so out of touch with reality, yet clearly so distressed all the time.

We discovered staff on the ward did not coerce her to eat or drink, if she refused. Once, we saw a consultant who told us she was much better – when we asked why she looked so yellow, as if jaundiced, I was sure he thought we were speaking about another patient.

Another time, John and I took her out of the hospital for a stroll in the park opposite. It was a lovely sunny day, and we sat on a bench together, with Mum at one end and me at the other. John got up to take a photo, and we promised to send her a copy. Looking at the photo on his laptop at home, he decided to edit the picture to show us sitting side by side. I sent the photo to her.

When I rang her after she had received it, she asked when he had taken the photo. I reminded her of our walk in the park, and she remembered it but said, "But you weren't sitting next to me."

"No, Mum," I replied. "He changed it on his computer."

I guessed what was coming.

"But he didn't have his computer with him!" she exclaimed. She could not get her head around that bit of technology.

Over the following months, her health deteriorated, and we spent several anxious days dashing to and from London as she got more and more poorly. She was a lifelong smoker and had respiratory failure, which, in the end, left her dependent on oxygen to keep her alive.

One sad day in 2001, we drove down to London knowing it was the last time I would see her. She had been admitted as an emergency to King's College Hospital, across the road from the Maudsley Hospital where she had spent the past six weeks. At the time of admission, she was found to have renal failure, malnutrition, a collapsed lung and was having a heart attack. She had been resuscitated twice before we got there, and we were called into a side room immediately.

I asked the young female doctor how she could have had all these severe conditions when she had been in a National Health Service hospital for over a month. She looked at me with tears in her eyes and shrugged. I always regret that after Mum's death I did not lodge a complaint with the mental hospital on my mum's behalf. Jim was not keen for me to make a fuss, and said they had cared for her for many years with dedication.

The nurse said, "Her lungs and kidneys are not working now. What do you want us to do?"

I realised with horror that she was asking us to decide on ending Mum's life. Despite the grave situation, it was difficult to comprehend that she was dying and had no time left. I looked at Jim and he shook his head.

We went to see her in intensive care. She was covered in tubes and breathing with a respirator. She removed the respirator tube by herself during the following night, and regained consciousness. When we visited, she recognised me, but was clearly confused and frightened. I told the nurse we did not want to prolong her suffering and that they should not resuscitate her again.

Jim asked me to make the sad decision to turn off her life support. He had said his goodbyes and could not face watching her fade away. I, alone, sat with her for her last hour, talking to her, and telling her I loved her and that we would take care of her husband. She squeezed my hand and slipped peacefully away. I felt immense sadness that her life had been so difficult.

My sister dashed down from her home in Manchester, but was too late to see her.

A week later, we two stood at her graveside and cried together for all that had been lost for her and us, and we promised to stay close. That closeness has grown over the years and we are great friends.

My sister had a much more traumatic time when she left the family in Shirley. She is now piecing together her story to make some sense of what happened all those years ago.

CHAPTER TWENTY-ONE

A New Role

My next career move took me to Derby, where I became the teacher in charge of a new diagnostic and assessment unit attached to a primary school. This followed on from the recent training I had taken in diagnostic assessment. A small group consisting of another teacher, four nursery nurses and I worked with children aged two to five years who had some form of developmental delay. It was really a good excuse to play! I loved working with these little ones.

We worked with educational psychologists and speech therapists to identify, through tests and the close observation of each child, any difficulties that the child was experiencing that were giving cause for concern. For example, one little boy of three joined us with many unexplained bruises. It would be usual to suspect abuse. However, what we observed was that he was falling a lot, and was not able to negotiate his way around the room full of toys and other children without bumping into them and tumbling. Alongside our observations, other disciplines would test for various conditions and we came to the conclusion – rightly, as it later turned out – that he had some form of muscular dystrophy. We became quite skilful as a team in noticing problems that had not yet been observed by others.

We worked closely with parents and encouraged them to look at their child's behaviour, and we talked about ways of coping at home. Children who were developing signs of autistic behaviour benefited from a small, closed environment where we could observe their interaction with others. Many of the children who had delayed development showed quick improvement when in a small group. We instigated a toy library for parents to borrow suitable toys to help their child at home.

The headteacher of the primary school to which we were attached was bemused and anxious about the diagnostic unit, which she declared had been 'foisted' on her, and about which she was very sceptical. "I don't know why the authorities have placed these children on our site," she once declared to me. "After all, it's not as if they will be able to go to a normal school, is it?"

The concept of the unit was to explore where the children might best be placed and most of them did, eventually, go to a 'normal' school.

I had been at the unit less than a year when a job was advertised that seemed too good not to go for. It was for a newly built, all-age special school on the outskirts of Derby, for children aged from two to nineteen years. I went for an interview, alongside a friend from my college days, and I got the job, somewhat to my amazement.

The interview was an experience in itself. There was a panel of two education officers, a Tory councillor who would be the chair of governors for the new school, a parent and a secretary taking notes. The female councillor sat opposite me, with her legs apart, showing her voluminous knickers. It was hard not to stare and harder still to concentrate on what she was saying.

One question from an education officer nearly flawed me. He asked me, "What does your husband think about you applying for this job?"

This was 1977, long before political correctness was widespread.

I thought quickly and replied, "Well, he will certainly enjoy the extra income." Had I blown it, I wondered?

When I was called back into the interview room, somewhat dazed, to realise I was being offered the job, the education officer came up to me and said, "Nearly got you then."

I thought it was a pretty low trick, but I was never nervous in his company again.

In the morning, before the interview, candidates were taken to the building site where the school was at foundations stage; it was just a muddy building site, really.

The day after my successful interview, I was taken back to my future school's site to have a more thorough look around.

The builders were interested to know who got the job. I blushed when I overheard the remark, "I told you the one with the legs would get it."

No one had ever made a comment about my legs before. However, over the next eleven months whilst I was waiting for the completion of my school, I had lots of banter and good humour with the builders whenever I went on site. I heard comments frequently about the lavish furnishings and speculation about what kind of children would be going there.

I was appointed in November 1997 to open the school the following September. I started the job in April to be able to interview and appoint over sixty staff, and to visit all of the ninety-plus families to introduce myself and tell them about the new school. My previous work with families was helpful for me to address their worries.

The building of the school went way beyond the estimated completion date and so, for the only occasion, in my career I had time to spare. I was allowed an unusual privilege, that of working with the architect and county advisers to design the interior of the whole building. This was very exciting, but very frustrating too. In one afternoon, I was expected to choose colour schemes for a building the size of several large houses, including bathroom tiles; the sizes of toilets for different age groups; and the wallpaper for my office. The latter was the only area for which the architect made his own choice. When my room was finished, I walked in to find a wall covered with jumping elephants and jungle creatures.

When I looked surprised, he said, "I looked at you and thought this was the most suitable."

And it was. It certainly helped to break the ice with visitors! There were times over the years when I did wish I could be in a jungle to escape the pressures. I lost count of the number of visitors who asked me why I chose that wallpaper, and children would wander in, perch cross-legged on the floor and make up a story about the animals.

The school was designed with a state-of-the-art gymnasium, with ropes, wall bars and a roll-out climbing frame. Despite recognising the luxury of such wonderful resources, I had to put my foot down to have more suitable, simple climbing apparatus for the needs of these children. I was often working with external advisers who had little or no concept of children with severe disabilities, and, as many teachers in these schools will tell you, you feel like you have to teach the whole community to understand and value the children as people.

On the other hand, I had to argue loudly for a piano. The architect tried to tell me that these children would not be able to take piano lessons, ignoring the fact that we might want a pianist to play to them. I was not able to stop the installation of a 'workshop' filled with a very expensive band saw, wood lathe and multiple sets of tools. We never had a teacher who was qualified to use any of this equipment. The best use made of this facility in my time at the school was for planting and growing seedlings, which an enterprising teacher helped pupils turn into hanging baskets to sell to parents and friends.

Because the children were aged from two to nineteen years, the secondary-school-age pupils attracted a budget for secondary-school resources – which were guarded closely by each specialist secondary-education adviser at the education department, as I later realised. Hence the lack of understanding between the county's advisers and me regarding woodwork, music, arts, physical education and home economics. It was not until I got to know my husband John, who was then a secondary-education adviser, that I found out how the politics of advisers guarding 'their' budgets really worked, but, by then, I was ten years into the job with a bit more wisdom.

Before the school opened, I started out on a mission to visit the adjacent secondary school to start to build a good relationship with its pupils and staff. I asked the headteacher if I could talk to class groups about the sort of children who were soon to be their neighbours. In the future years, it would prove most advantageous to get to know staff and pupils at the seven other schools on the same road as ours, for purposes of integration. When I spoke to the headmaster of the secondary school, he agreed to my proposal readily, but said that – in order to get through to the children attending that school – I would need to speak to fourteen class groups. *Well,* I thought, *here goes.*

The experience was enlightening. The children came into the classroom looking hostile and bored. I organised them into groups and started by asking them all the words they knew for a mentally handicapped person. They were startled, and I had their attention. With much embarrassed giggling, they got involved. We then went on to have an animated discussion about the labels we give each other, how it feels and what we mean by 'normal'. I finished each session by asking them not to label the children who would be attending our school next door, but to befriend them by coming inside to help when they could. This led, in the end, to a very productive programme of lunchtime support by those young people for individual children in our school, which lasted many years – and I never felt the need to repeat my awareness sessions.

The relationships between the two schools were usually positive. I was very excited and energised by the prospect of this new venture – it was a chance to do good things, I hoped, for some very special children.

CHAPTER TWENTY-TWO

Choosing My Team

As explained in the previous chapter, I actually started my new job in April 1977 with nowhere to go, as the new school building was not finished. I was allowed to take up a space in the committee room at the education office in the city, which was the very room where I had had the interview for the job. This was a first for the staff working there. I got to know the officers, the transport team, the advisers, the psychologists and the school meals teams, and, more importantly, they got to know me, so that whenever we had a problem subsequently with transport arrangements for the children or school meals I could ring and talk to my 'old friends'. They were a great bunch of people.

My first appointment to the new school was for a school secretary, since I needed someone to help with the volume of paperwork ahead of me. I interviewed Iris, who joined me, and we sat at the long, polished committee table on her first day, armed only with two notepads and pens – which I had nipped out to buy before she arrived.

She said, "What do we do first, boss?"

So, we went out and found the nearest place for lunch. That was the start of St Andrew's School, and a wonderful long relationship with a brilliant school secretary.

Iris was a wonderful secretary. She was always kind, caring, hard-working and a great support to me. The children all loved her and popped in to see her when they escaped from class. The teaching staff equally recognised what a gem she was – and put upon her mercilessly from time to time. I often had to say to her, "Don't say yes to everybody's workload." But she always did, and they loved her for it. She loved her shiny, new electric typewriter and was not too happy when a computer was introduced into her office. She continued to use the electric typewriter and the old-fashioned copying machine as long as she could. I, too, was trying to learn how to operate a computer, as the job required more and more reports and information for parents, psychologists, speech therapists, school governors and the Department for Education in London.

I was obviously very involved with my work; it was a huge challenge, and I was just thirty-three. I had so much to plan and think about. It was hard on my husband Patrick and my teenage son Shaun. My mind was often occupied with planning and thinking about the job. It was a very satisfying job, but, to my surprise, it was also very lonely. The kind of camaraderie that I had enjoyed at the small school in Ashbourne with a dozen children and a few staff could not be achieved in this large organisation. For me, this was the beginning of difficulties, which would surface many years later. It is hard to be a working wife and mother, and to be successful in each role.

My husband was always very supportive. He believed that I should use my talents and he was proud of my success. I was working in a job he knew nothing about, and so trying to share my anxieties with him was difficult. He would jokingly say, "Playing with kids; how difficult can that be? And you've got a secretary."

I know he was teasing partly to relieve my anxiety, but the pressures ultimately took their toll on us all. I always put pressure on myself by wanting everything to be perfect.

To find all the new teachers and support staff we needed, I undertook a mammoth interviewing schedule. I had help from a number of education officers and advisers, and we managed to gather together a diverse team of people who were all passionate about the new venture. I had to declare to them as a group what my philosophy would be. Wow! I stayed awake a lot worrying over the correct words. In reality I simply said that the school was all about people, but first and foremost always about the children, and that – with such a magnificent building – we had an opportunity to do things really differently with these young people.

Many of the teachers and assistants had little or no experience with children with multiple disabilities, so I was a trainer initially, as well as a boss. Some of the teachers were transferred from another school in the city that had very different values and ethos; initially, they were sceptical and resistant to everything I suggested. The outcome was, largely, a team with very dynamic and interesting ideas and personalities. I realised I was on probation in their eyes.

The first day the school opened was chaotic; it was also my birthday. The education department insisted that we admit all the children on day one, and I agreed. Years later, I learned from experienced headteachers that was most unusual for a new school, and I could have insisted on staggering the intake of pupils over a period of time.

The children were very excited on arrival; they had not seen the school before, some were starting school for the first time, and some had a condition that required a familiar, quiet environment with very skilled management. All of them were travelling with strangers that first day. As the children – all ninety-six of them – tumbled out of buses and taxis, one child had a fit in the school entrance and another ran off. Getting everybody into the right rooms was a mammoth task.

The school provided education for children aged from two to nineteen years in four departments. Within the first hour, I learned that all the toilets were blocked – with builders' rubble. Furniture was not in the correct rooms. The taxi escorts did not have all the children's names or addresses. The kitchen staff were short of many essential items for cooking the meals, and – when I went to the kitchen to enquire why adults were being given tiny cutlery to eat with – I nearly got my head bitten off by the cook.

I had a somewhat dynamic relationship with the school cook, who challenged me a lot. She would frequently pop her head around my open door and ask, "Anita, dear, what are you going to do about...?" She and I developed a good working relationship and came to understand our roles better, and her commitment to the children made her a firm friend. She was very sad when I left sixteen years later.

We got through that first day of drama somehow, even though my day and every other day in the following weeks lasted into late evening. But our school was underway.

⎯⎯ ✦ ⎯⎯

We had two opening ceremonies. The first was a visit from Mike Yarwood, comedian, who was at that time a national figure on television. We learned a bit about the problems with celebrity: he arrived very late, and we had to keep all the children at school way past their home time; he rushed around posing for photographs with a false smile, and disappeared after twenty minutes and a few hasty autographs. "Was that it?" I heard up and down the corridors.

The second 'official' ceremony was equally bizarre and was attended by the large Tory councillor who had interviewed me with her knickers on show. To her credit, she showed me her nicer side on this occasion, by asking me if I thought her hat looked a bit ridiculous. Well, what do you say? I needed to keep my job.

A shiny, brass plate was fixed to a wall in our school hall – which is one of the perks of local government.

CHAPTER TWENTY-THREE

New Ways

WHEN THE SCHOOL OPENED, A GROUP OF CHILDREN WERE
transferred from another school. They came with no records, but just
a word-of-mouth assessment of their capabilities. Many had been
introduced to reading books, and I was told there were some good
readers amongst them.

Some parents thought we would be teaching subjects such as
reading and numbers in formal ways; that is, getting the children to
sit still and learn by rote. I had lots of 'discussions' about the needs
of the children and the sequences of learning at the child's levels of
ability. I insisted we begin with an intensive round of assessment
for every child, to be sure what their capabilities and problems
were. I received no records from their previous school and much
of their previous education had been planned around guesswork;
it reminded me of my days of basketmaking and needlework. For
children with such diverse and complex needs, it was crucial that
we knew at what levels they were functioning. Some parents think
that if you teach a child in traditional ways – even in a mainstream
classroom – they will be more normal and learn from the other
children. It is a hard learning curve for some families and, sadly,
many see the 'special school' as a last resort. I must add that many
children do now succeed in mainstream primary schools, secondary

schools and even at college, with the right support. We were always concerned for the most vulnerable ones.

We purchased remedial reading and writing materials, and I led the development of an assessment procedure. We had to sell this to the parents who believed their children were much more able than our observations told us. Anyone who has read a favourite story to a toddler will know that they soon know all the words, can 'read' each page with you and tell you when you pretend to go wrong. A number of the children who were said to be readers were, in fact, at this stage. Whilst we had many books of all kinds in our library, and we soon received the services of the excellent schools' library service, those children who were ready certainly progressed to more formal reading lessons. I felt that sitting a child in front of a book and pretending to parents that the child was reading with understanding was wrong. It took a long time to get that message over to both staff and parents. Instead, I wanted to emphasise the importance of learning through play. Not least because these children needed a vehicle to develop their language and social behaviour. It seemed to me that both we and the parents needed to focus on their child's independence for the future, which was then – and still is – a source of great worry, since there are limited options for the care of these children after their parents are no longer there.

Many of the teaching and support staff were wonderfully inspiring in the ways they found to interest and engage the children in learning – particularly through music, drama, stories and language development – even though the parents and governors sometimes could not understand the purpose and methods we were applying. One interesting result of our concentration on helping children develop independence was that they became more assertive with their parents who began to complain that their child was less manageable at home. This led to parents having to change their ways too – which was not an easy message to take on board.

Gradually, I introduced parents' evenings, where we could discuss – individually and in small groups – what we were aiming for in the way we were teaching their children, but it took a while for parents to gain confidence in the school's methods.

There was little material around to help with creating a suitable curriculum for these children, who had many complex difficulties. Social activities were important, as was individual speech therapy, which was supported by a therapist who came into the school several times a week. As a whole school, we were persuaded to use a sign language system called Makaton, which was new to schools. Every member of staff, including me, had to attend in-school training, and we encouraged all staff to use signing to all children as a communication system that could help children. One teacher – Kathy, who worked with parents – was our expert. She used Makaton all the time – much to the amusement of her family at home.

Parents also received training – when they could be persuaded to come to sessions. The common response was, "My child doesn't need to sign; he [or she] can already speak."

I had to explain that signing was an aid to talking fluently, and that children needed to speak to each other. In due course, this proved to be the case, and it was an immense help for children who could not talk. I am pleased to see actors using Makaton on CBBC television these days.

One day, a head of department in the senior school came to me and told me that a youngster was to go into hospital and was very frightened. She asked, "May we create a 'hospital' in the classroom?"

Knowing her creative skills, I agreed to her proposal that for the next whole week, the classrooms would be structured so that the young people could get some ideas of what going into hospital would be like. When it was all set up, I went to see. There was a reception desk for appointments and clinics – one of the pupils was pretending to make appointments and answering the telephone. There was a ward for patients on beds (using tables), with stethoscopes, gowns and masks loaned from a staff member's doctor father. There was a bandaging area, with a child as the nurse bandaging a 'patient' by wrapping the bandage over the body and under the table. Teachers supplied white coats and nurses' uniforms, a thermometer, plasters, swabs, pretend syringes and a host of aids to represent a hospital. The teenagers loved it, and their speech and understanding came on in leaps and bounds. They talked of nothing else for weeks. The youngster went to hospital and recovered well, with less anxiety.

The parents of the children must have wondered who this nutcase was who had taken command of their child's education. Sometimes, they let me know what they thought in no uncertain terms, but many told me how their child was better behaved at home, more able to communicate and happier.

On another occasion, a teacher was getting married, and it became apparent that most of the children had never been to a real wedding. We decided to hold a mock wedding ceremony, and everybody rose to the occasion. The local vicar came and conducted the 'service', complete with many bridesmaids in pretty dresses; the school's deputy head was the groom; and there was confetti and a wedding cake, which was provided by our school cook. Again, this prompted a lot of conversation and spin-off activities with the children.

The senior school had a large kitchen with a fully furnished area for small group dining. Groups of pupils – known as 'students' after age sixteen – could learn to go shopping then prepare a meal, entertain their friends, and learn home skills such as washing up, cleaning and food preparation – all in a reasonably real-life setting.

Ultimately, some children progressed to asking their parents for a shopping list and going to shop at a local supermarket. They also learned how to prepare home-made soup, and sold it to staff and visitors at lunchtimes, or to groups of parents who had been invited in. This was a great opportunity to demonstrate to parents what their child could do, if encouraged. Most said they would not have dreamed of giving their son or daughter so much responsibility.

The same groups of pupils had lesson times devoted to learning how to tidy and clean the homemaking areas, increasing their independence at home in preparation for the future.

Next, let me tell you about the school's sex education. The government decreed that sex education should be part of the curriculum of all secondary schools, but did not provide any strategies or advice as to how we teachers in special schools might deliver it.

A weekend training course was arranged for special-school headteachers in the county's residential training centre. I went along. The county adviser for special education was responsible for planning and coordinating the two-day course. He looked anxious and bemused as we arrived, which was most unusual for this friendly, easy-going Liverpudlian.

The course was different from the annual lecturing style, to say the least. The course was run by marriage-guidance specialists, including a sex therapist. With little introduction, we were shown a series of videos of explicit sexual activities, each followed by workshops in small groups to discuss our reactions to the films. This was supposed to introduce us and desensitize us to the range of human behaviours, and help us to promote the topic in our schools. Most of us felt nervous about exposing our views to other headteachers, whom we barely knew. The county adviser looked visibly shaken after the first morning and shared his anxiety that the county politicians would be outraged to think we were watching 'sex films' on ratepayers' money and in work time. I'm not sure the course did much for me except perhaps give me confidence to talk to parents and staff.

The room in which the films were shown had a door off a corridor with a window in it. Outside the room were a group of decorators painting the corridor, except they weren't; they were watching the films, with much noise and laughter. Our trainers, red-faced, rushed to cover the window with a sheet of paper. The comments of the painters about headteachers of today were entertaining. However, the leaders feared an item appearing in the *News of the World* if the wrong word got out about the course. Or even worse if the council's elected members got wind of it. The workmen probably had a new respect for teachers – or maybe not.

The topic was received with enthusiasm at my school because the staff had become aware increasingly of the inappropriate sexualised behaviour of some of our pupils. This had led to some difficult situations, not least for some of the young teaching assistants who were just a few years older than the pupils concerned. We were able to discuss strategies on how to cope with overt 'natural' behaviours, such as masturbation, which others might indulge in privately, but which were occurring in classrooms or when out in the community. We talked about what would constitute unacceptable behaviours too – some were clearly not acceptable as part of normal growing up. Finding ways to talk to our pupils about such issues was explored.

Subsequently, I organised a series of meetings with parents of different age groups in the school to discuss this delicate topic, with a variety of reactions, but – in the main – the parents were pleased that we were prepared to talk to their children about such things without embarrassment.

This was except for one elderly couple who were the parents of a seventeen-year-old boy, and had asked to meet me in private. They came to me looking very frosty and uncomfortable. One of them explained, "We don't want you to talk about such things to our son, R. We think you will just give him ideas. He has Down's syndrome, so he couldn't possibly understand such things, and, anyway, he never goes anywhere without us, so there won't be any problems. May he be excused from these lessons?"

When I asked them about their son's life at home, it became clear that he had no privacy or freedom to make any decisions. They conceded that he had started touching himself, but they told him off and he seemed to have stopped.

I knew that some staff were having difficulties with R's behaviour in class, which was very much focussed on girls. He would often expose himself and masturbate in the classroom. He was very affectionate toward the girls and staff, but was not aware when his attentions were unwanted, which led to distressing situations. He often tried to kiss and cuddle them in ways that were embarrassing for others. He kept telling one particular girl that he was going to marry her. He had very little speech, but could understand instructions if given to him in simple sentences. Whilst his teachers were coping, and avoiding the topic, they were not helping him to understand where and when such behaviour was appropriate, and the meaning of a private place – which was something he clearly never had. We had to comply with his parents' wishes to exclude him from sex education lessons.

A few weeks later, I got a call from the young man's older brother to ask if he could come and talk to me. He was concerned, and told us that he had heard the story bit by bit from his reluctant parents and that what they had told me had been wrong. He proceeded to tell me that his brother, who was two years younger than him, was increasingly showing sexualised behaviour in very inappropriate ways. He had exposed himself to relatives. He masturbated a lot and in front of his parents. He had started to have temper outbursts, having been a mild, obedient boy until then. The picture he painted was so different to that from his parents. He begged me to give his brother access to advice about how to manage his feelings.

What a thoughtful, caring brother.

He went on to say that he was urging his parents to let his brother grow up and do normal teenage things with a bit more independence.

I suggested that, firstly, his parents should arrange for his brother to have privacy. Secondly, they should listen to what he was trying to say. Thirdly, they should not to be afraid of him growing into an adult, with normal emotions and needs.

He went away with ideas to put to his parents and the situation improved in time.

Fortunately, by this time, the school had the addition of a residential wing for pupils to stay in during the week to learn some independence and to give their parents a much-needed break. R was admitted, and his life changed. He became a happy, mature teenager with friends amongst the other teenagers – he even had a girlfriend. His parents told me eventually how grateful they were that we had stepped in and taught their son how to manage his developing sexuality. This kind of situation was not uncommon. Each success gave us the courage to believe it was the right way to go.

Another teenage girl, who was living alone with her sixty-year-old widowed father began to show highly sexualised behaviour in class with the boys. She talked about having a bath with her dad who she said was going to marry her, and she described how he would rub her and say naughty things that she must not tell anybody about. The teachers were seriously concerned because she could not have learned this behaviour by chance, nor from any other child in class.

We were advised to keep notes by her social worker and, in the end, a child-protection case conference was called. There was a degree of scepticism around the room about what I was saying. Of course, it was difficult for the conference members to decide if what the child was saying and doing was real or fantasy.

A specialist worker experienced in work with abused children was employed to sit with the pupil and to explore issues with her using anatomical dolls, which the child would be able to use to demonstrate what she knew through play. Questions would be asked of her about bedtime, bath time, etc. through the dolls. The outcome was to confirm the probability of some sexual activity.

No action was taken, as it was normal to err on the side of the perpetrator. In this case it was possible to believe that a lonely man, who was recently widowed, was seeking some form of relief, albeit inappropriate, with his daughter.

We now know from revelations about child abuse that many children and young people with learning difficulties are subjected to abuse, with their abusers believing that they cannot explain what has been done to them. In helping these young people to better understand appropriate behaviours, we hoped we were protecting them from being so easily taken advantage of.

I began to be involved in joint child-protection meetings with the social services, health and police authorities, as the scale of the issues were slowly emerging.

What has also become more widely appreciated is the need for people with disabilities – including those with learning difficulties – to have normal, fulfilling lives and friendships, and that these can help them move toward managing to live independently when they are adults, as well as allowing them to experience loving relationships just like anybody else.

On the other hand, helping teenagers to become more independent often raised tricky situations at home, since they were no longer content to sit in a corner and be docile, but showed some of the typical teenage behaviours.

In the 1970s, when people challenged us about our responsibility to protect these vulnerable people, I remember saying, "Never underestimate what these young people can achieve with the right support. They constantly surprise us."

Recently, I read about two people with Down's syndrome who have been married for twenty-five years. They have looked after each other and had a very happy marriage. How different from the days when such people were shut away at home, out of sight, or worse, locked away in a remote subnormality hospital.

I recently met a woman called Chris at the bus station. In talking about writing, she shared with me the story of her son, who had Down's syndrome and had recently died. In his short life, he had achieved a Duke of Edinburgh's Award and had attended the local grammar school – my own old school.

I was once asked to give a talk to a group of teachers and educational psychologists about the role of play in children's development. Knowing that they were a fairly cynical bunch, I started with an unusual activity. I gave out a number of kiddies' bubble blowers and asked the audience to blow bubbles. Of course, there was chaos and much enjoyment, but I had made my point – we all like to play and learn best when we are happily engaged.

From the beginning of the life of St Andrew's School, we established a role for a teacher trained in counselling, who would visit parents at home and, if necessary, accompany them into school for meetings. This was a valuable way for us to develop a working partnership with parents. Their stories were often heartrending: stories of feeling bewildered about their child's condition and being unable to find information that could help them bring up their child. We urged parents to try, as far as possible, to treat their child in the same way as their other children, by encouraging good behaviour, etc. and taking them out to experience normal things. Everyday life for them was often a great trial, especially in public.

I remember one occasion when a parent observed her daughter, aged seven, eating her lunch at a table with others. She was sitting still and taking turns as requested.

Her mother said, "How did you get her to do that? She won't sit down at home. She throws her food about and has a tantrum when she can't get her own way. She often stands on the table, screaming, and ruins the meal for everyone."

I asked her carefully if her other daughter, aged two years, did that too.

She said that they did not allow her to because she was a 'normal child', and she had to learn good table manners, but that they had to make exceptions for this one because of her problems.

I thought for a bit and replied, "What will happen if she is still doing this when she is a teenager?"

The mother replied that would not happen. Almost before I could ask the next question, she stated, "I suppose we ought to make rules and stick to them now, whilst she is young and we can lift her off the table."

I was reminded of this issue when I saw my infant grandchild throwing a tantrum and saw his good behaviour chart on the wall.

We encouraged some parents who were clearly exhausted by the round-the-clock care of their child to consider occasional residential relief. The child would gain as much as the parents from going away for a weekend to a home for such children, where their needs were understood. This was a hard message to sell, and parents often struggled on until a crisis made a period away from home inevitable.

The local authority opened a new respite-care house on the outskirts of the city, and we were able to obtain some places for individual families to send their child for a weekend or during the school holidays.

We also provided a toy library from which parents could borrow appropriate toys for their child, and be given guidance on how to play with and stimulate them.

During the long summer break – which is always a difficult time for many parents, but more so for those with a disabled child – we organised a summer school, with the help of some staff and many volunteers. This provided a whole range of outdoor activities, as well as activities in school, and this scheme was very much appreciated by parents.

CHAPTER TWENTY-FOUR

Fun and Games

I WAS ALWAYS INTERESTED IN DEVELOPING CREATIVE activities with the children because I could see how music, drama and language-related activities enabled children to learn, and helped those who were hyperactive, shy or cut off from normal means of communication.

In the early 1980s, we were fortunate enough to have a week-long workshop from the Interplay Community Theatre group based in Leeds. When their team came to plan the event, they explained it would all be part of an unfolding story as the days went by. The story they planned to develop concerned a large papier mâché whale, which they had constructed and which would disgorge a new character each day. There would be spin-off activities for each class during every day and a whole school sing-song before the children went home. The children and adults would be dressed up, and all of us, me included, would take part. I did not have a problem in selling this to the staff, they had come to accept my wacky ideas in the main, and it promised a change from classroom teaching. They understood immediately how this approach might reach some of our profoundly disabled young people.

I arrived at school early the following Monday to find that the players had constructed a large pool filled with water on the lovely wooden floor of the gym. When the children arrived, they were led into the hall and were excited by the notion of something exciting happening.

The week was a wonderful success and produced many spin-off activities, new songs and new friendships. The last day began with a message to say that the whale had been stolen, and we all must rush out to find it. Coaches waited outside to take all the children and staff to hunt for the whale. The local policeman was primed to do his bit in telling the children which way to go.

We set off and, in time, arrived at the planned destination: the gardens of a stately home. I had been asked by the players to agree to be tied to a statue in the garden, so that the children on their search could be told a bit more of the story by me. As I waited, I saw a gentleman in evening dress appear at the end of the avenue.

He sauntered along, stopped when he saw me and said, "I must have had a lot to drink last night. Who are you?"

There was nothing for it but to come clean. "Well, I'm actually a headteacher. I'm helping some children find a whale."

"I think I need to lie down," was all he said.

At the end of the search was a returned whale and a celebration dance in the courtyard – it was a truly unique experience.

The group returned again a few years later and created a castle in the school hall with similar activities and enjoyment for the children. The parents complained that they were not able to come into school to watch the events.

—∞—

Three further events stand out in my memory. The first being a series of workshops at the school from the Manchester Symphony Orchestra. The musicians had never worked with such severely disabled children before. They brought various instruments into school – a harp, a trombone, drums and a double bass – and they helped the children to gain an experience of real music-making. We had a good variety of percussion instruments in school with which the group were able to introduce simple rhythms and create jazz pieces. It was amazing to watch their skill at engaging each child.

I remember seeing a tiny child lying at the side of the harp to catch the vibrations. Another child who was deaf put his face to the bass and felt the instrument's movement – his smile was beautiful.

Toward the end of the series of workshops, we were invited to go with a group of our children to Cheethams in Manchester to show off our performances alongside other schools at a special schools' concert.

Another memorable event was when the school was awarded a National Award for Curriculum Innovation, as a result of the sort of activities I have described. A group of pupils, parents and staff travelled with me to collect the award at the Barbican in London, along with young people from special schools around the country. The main event was very long, with lots of speeches, and was fairly boring for the children, unfortunately. The organisers had thought only of the important people giving speeches and not much about the needs of hundreds of disabled children sitting for two hours in a hot, dark theatre. However, the experiences of travelling by train to London, staying in student accommodation, making their own breakfasts, dressing up and travelling on the Tube were what they remembered best for a long time afterwards.

We decided to organise an outdoor adventure holiday with a difference. The education authority funded an outdoor-pursuits centre in beautiful, rugged countryside north of Buxton in the Peak District. I had the idea of furthering cooperation between our school and the neighbouring comprehensive school by organising a joint adventure week for teenagers from both schools, with their respective staff. This was to be a residential week, and we chose children who had already had some experience of being away from home.

I accompanied a teacher from the comprehensive school to a planning meeting at the outdoor-pursuits centre, full of confidence in what we were about to embark on. When the qualified instructors at the centre began to understand the nature of the pupils we were taking, they became extremely uncooperative and declared that it would not work. They said things like, "Those sort of children will be a liability. They will hold the 'normal' children back. It will be too dangerous. What if something goes wrong?" On and on went their excuses for not taking the plunge, but they reckoned without my determination.

When we returned to school, I approached one of those helpful county advisers and got him on side by convincing him that I would send enough staff so that the children would be well protected from danger and that any child could opt out of an activity if it did not feel safe or appropriate to let them have a go.

We won. We went. We and the children had a wonderful time.

Which children showed the most determination, courage, enjoyment and stickability? Ours, of course. Long after the comprehensive school's children had given up on sailing because they were cold, ours were still battling on. I was amazed at some of the activities they took part in and enjoyed: zip wires, potholing, abseiling, canoeing and night walks were just a few.

We, the teachers, had to join in everything too. I recall shouts from the youngsters of, "Your turn first, Anita."

Abseiling was a particular horror for me, but I put on a brave face and wobbled over the edge of the ridge like a geriatric.

Going down a cave on our stomachs, Peter, a plump sixteen-year-old who was ahead of me said, "I'm stuck, Anita."

"No, you're not," I responded, his muddy boots just in front of my nose. I had a fear of confined spaces as well. "Just keep reaching forward." Step by step, with much encouragement, I got through.

Peter declared, "See, you can do it, Anita. Good girl!"

Every evening, after the young people were in bed – they were asleep as soon as their heads touched the pillow, so tired were they – the centre staff had a debriefing meeting. The experts acknowledged the children's performance grudgingly at first, but, by the end of the week, they were as enthusiastic about this unique experience as we were.

Our pupils' parents were pretty impressed too and the children's confidence took a leap forward.

Repeating this venture in later times was more easily accepted. The children were always up for it and would ask me every day when I went into their classrooms, "What's happening today?" Many teachers would envy such enthusiasm for learning.

All the musicians, actors and artists who came into the school had a great empathy with the children, especially those with multiple of the most profound disabilities. Watching a member of the group carrying a little one around whilst playing the flute or a seasoned climber helping a child by placing limbs gently was very moving.

Judy, a blind teacher, came to give singing and music sessions to groups of pupils at the school. We had a personal connection: she had married Ian, the boy next door from my childhood in Shirley village. She had a degree in music and a very lively, interesting personality. Her role was to teach music to groups of children through singing and using percussion, piano and guitar.

Accompanying her at the time was her equally intelligent and lively working dog – a labradoodle called Barney. Barney was always perfectly well behaved when in his harness, but he became a delinquent out of it. He would sit in the staffroom at lunchtime and remove the sandwiches of the staff quietly whilst they fussed over him.

Judy would be alerted by the giggles around and would say sternly, "Barney, what are you doing? What's he up to?"

His ears would droop and a sad expression usually sufficed for him to be forgiven.

Once, he wandered along a corridor past a group of small children, saw the little snowmen they had carefully constructed and displayed on a shelf, and helped himself to several of them. The children shrieked, and he put one back.

He was much loved by the whole school. When he was not on duty guiding Judy, he would keep Iris company in the office hoping for a sneaky biscuit.

In the early 1980s, a national debate was developing about children with disabilities being allowed to go to their local junior or senior schools. There was great pressure from parents' groups to see their children educated in 'normal' schools. Despite their satisfaction at their children's progress in a special school, like all parents, they wanted their child to mix with others and have the opportunity to make friends in their own locality. The stigma of going to a special school was cited as a reason for going to the local school, as was the opportunity to study real subjects, and, it was implied, become more 'normalised'. Others argued that many of our children would not cope with the busy environment of a junior school, and even less the curriculum of a secondary school.

However, it was a time of change, and there was much discussion nationally about the school curriculum and what it should contain. At my school, we had begun recently to take individual children and small groups into the primary and secondary schools that were sited conveniently adjacent to our school. Careful preparation by teachers in both schools, as well as with the children, made sure of success.

The children were integrated in physical education classes, art classes and swimming sessions to begin with. One girl with Down's syndrome gained a GCE in art in one year as a result of this work, proving that some integration was certainly possible.

CHAPTER TWENTY-FIVE

A New Son

AT THAT TIME, MY HUSBAND PATRICK AND I HAD NOT planned for another baby since I had such a demanding job, but the news that I was pregnant – which came on his fortieth birthday – was very welcome. In September 1980, my second son, David was born. He had a head of dark hair and was a good, quiet baby.

During my labour, I received three messages from a man, who was not my husband. It turned out to be my deputy at school, who was being urged by my school staff to ring to enquire about my progress every half hour or so. This caused me a little embarrassment with the nurses.

This time, I was able to take maternity leave and I very much enjoyed the six months I had at home with David. I realised, sadly, that I was most content, relaxed and happy when I stayed at home looking after my little ones. My husband and I never had any discussion about whether I could or should give up my job.

Before I returned to work, we found Jane – a beautiful, talented, trained nursery nurse – who was to spend the next few years helping us to look after our baby in our home. This was an excellent arrangement because David remained in a familiar environment, and Jane could ring me anytime there was a problem. She was always patient and full of humour, and we became good friends and have remained so, even though David is now thirty-five and has two sons of his own. Without her, I could not have managed to stay in my job.

I returned to work in March 1981 and was plunged immediately into plans for building a new residential wing and two staff houses on site. The pressure never seemed to stop and, although I was still enjoying the job, the sleepless nights at home took their toll. I never seemed to get a full night's sleep.

Then, in 1984, there began a period of acrimonious industrial action by the teaching unions across the country, with teachers in my school refusing to look after the children at lunchtime and refusing to attend after-school meetings for their own training and development. These were very stressful times, and I felt that the nature of the school and education in general was changing. I heard that one teacher had been pinned against a wall by the union rep until she promised to support the strike action, which she definitely did not believe in. The strike action was very divisive. On the one hand, I was advised not to be provocative toward the strike nor stop teachers from taking part; on the other hand, I had parents calling anxiously to ask if their children would be looked after properly at all times.

The education authority, which was very left wing at that time, called a meeting at the school and told me in front of the staff that I was being unreasonable in asking teachers not to strike in recognition of the special needs of the pupils. The left-wing chair of the school governors told me he did not believe schools needed a headteacher and they could manage very well without me. I was mortified at his manner and lack of support, with no recognition of all that I had achieved so far. I should have known better.

On the first day his party won the election and he was nominated as my chair of governors, he walked into my office unannounced, addressed me by my surname in a rude manner and said, "I'll be watching everything you do. I want a copy of every document and letter that you send out of this school – no cover-ups."

I was staggered. Overnight, when I had cooled down, I thought of a plan. The next day I began to send him a copy of every piece of information leaving the school, every letter, every note to parents about their child's wet nappy, every order for supplies and much, much more.

After a few days he phoned me and enquired, "Anita, what the **** are you playing at sending me all this rubbish?"

I reminded him calmly, with a straight face, of his instruction.

"I don't want all this ******* rubbish; you can stop sending it," he declared.

There's more than one way to skin a rabbit, I thought.

Fortunately, he did not challenge me on the education we provided – he would not have known the value of what we were doing. When we interviewed for new teachers, he was always there, writing notes on the proverbial fag packet. He tried to insist that we chose a candidate based purely on whether they supported his political party, which he somehow deduced from their answers. I had to argue rationally and calmly for the candidate whose knowledge and ideas most fitted the job.

This was a hard time for me. I knew very little about politics. I thought political pressure had no place in such a school, but I soon learned that all my fellow headteachers in the surrounding area were having just as difficult time. I found it hard to cope. My husband John – who was head of a secondary school at that time, which was before I knew him – says that he felt the antagonism from the politicians too, and it gave him sleepless nights, just like me.

It passed eventually and we all settled down to the routines of day-to-day life again.

CHAPTER TWENTY-SIX

Changing Times and a Trip to Italy

IN JULY 1986, I WAS GIVEN A SABBATICAL YEAR OFF TO study the impact of integrating disabled children into mainstream schools. I was based at Nottingham University with a professor who had an interest in children with Down's syndrome. Through him, I got the opportunity to travel to Italy, where a model of integrated learning was attracting international attention.

I flew to Naples and stayed with a family with two children. The mother was English, the father was French, and they spoke a mixture of these two languages plus Italian in the home. Their daughter, who had Down's syndrome, was aged seven at the time. She spoke a mixture of all three languages and would slip into another when she could not find a word in the language she had been speaking.

Once, explaining something to me in Italian, which I was struggling to understand, with hands on hips and wagging her finger, she said, "Anita, *tu e stupido!*" ("Anita, you are stupid!")

She was right; my language skills were not equal to hers.

It proved to me that teaching languages to young children and to disabled children was not only possible but could be helpful for their development. Our two-year-old grandson, when asked to sing a song, bursts forth with 'Frère Jacques' in a broad Lancashire accent. His mum is a language teacher. I believe he is getting an excellent introduction to foreign languages at the right age.

Whilst I was in Naples, the experience of sitting in on case conferences to talk about a particular child's development with parents, psychologists and teachers was tremendous, and my Italian improved in leaps and bounds. I was able to go into schools for children at nursery-, junior- and secondary-school ages.

The system in Italy at that time was that classes were of no more than twenty children and would include disabled children from the local area, plus a dedicated teacher for that child. Whilst the true social mixing of children was amazing – the disabled child was treated like all the others – the curriculum on offer and the lessons were not at all suitable for the disabled child's level of difficulty. Sometimes, children had to repeat a year thus losing the friendships they had gained already. So, it was not ideal, but there were interesting lessons to take back home.

When I returned to my school at the end of the summer of 1987, I wrote a paper on integration for the education department, and encouraged my teachers to forge further links with mainstream schools. We had some wonderful responses from parents and teachers in both types of schools. The local education authority was indifferent to my report – one adviser stated it was before its time. I think that, politically, integration was still in its early stages of development. I got some criticism from other special-school headteachers, who said I was trying to do away with my own job and theirs. I had never suggested or thought that all children with disabilities could or should go to a mainstream school. That is still the case nearly thirty years on, with special schools – including my own – flourishing and growing, particularly with the expertise needed to care for children with autism and other complex needs.

On my return to the school after my sabbatical, I was managing a small child and a teenager, and we moved between the residential house on the school site and our home in Ashbourne, at weekends when I was not on call.

I received a call one day about my foster parent Tom, whom I had seen only rarely in recent years, although he did share Christmas dinner with us each year. He was in a bad way and living alone in a council flat in the village of Brailsford, where I went to school as a junior. He had developed dementia and was still driving his Morris Minor to the football matches at Derby County. He had suffered a minor accident and was found wandering at night on a main road; he had lost all sense of where he was.

I went to see him, and he seemed to recognise me and agreed to go to see his GP. I rashly offered to have him with us for a while, since there was no residential care available. He stayed with us for a few weeks, but he was so disorientated and I worried about him constantly whilst I was working.

Eventually, his doctor had him admitted to a mental unit at the psychiatric hospital, and he stayed there until his death in early 1989. I visited him regularly, and he begged me to take him home. It was a sad ending for him, with no real friends or relatives to look out for him.

I organised his funeral and was astonished when a nephew of his appeared. I had never seen or heard anything about him since I was a small child. He asked coyly if his uncle had left any money or a will, and astounded me by declaring, "Well, he was nothing to you and he was my uncle, so I'm entitled to whatever he left."

Disgusted, I gave him the funeral bill and showed him the door. Poor Tom had never earned enough money to satisfy Doris, and he certainly had no pension.

I was becoming more and more stressed, and less efficient, at home and at work, although there was nobody I felt I could turn to who might understand and give me support. The introduction of the national curriculum in all the new subjects and key stages was upon us. I heard, with incredulity, at a headteachers' meeting that we were expected to introduce and teach all the new syllabuses to all age groups starting from day one. As I and my staff went to training sessions, we all became more and more horrified at the lack of understanding of the children's capabilities and their disabilities. Teachers were becoming rebellious. Many special schools took the line of wait and see how all these new subjects would shake down for our special children. So, in the summer of 1993, I was unprepared for the blast from the education department in London. No one had ever contacted me from there before.

The conversation went thus:

"It has come to my notice that you are late in submitting twelve written pieces of English work from your Key Stage 2 pupils. Why is this?" asked the man from the education department.

I gasped and, rapidly taking in what he was saying, replied, "We do not have any children who could complete these assignments."

"Do you have children in that age group?" he asked in a frosty, posh tone.

"We have three children aged fourteen," I stated. "None of them can read, one is blind, and two have hearing problems and epilepsy; they are functioning like small children."

"Do you mean to say that such children are educated in schools?" he queried.

"Of course, and they have been since the Education Act of 1972," I confirmed. How could he be so ignorant?

"Well, perhaps we could allow you to submit just one piece of written work for each child in the circumstances." With that, he rang off.

I put the phone down, put my head in my hands and sighed. At that moment, I knew that my career had to come to an end. I did not have enough fight left in me to plead against this steamroller called the national curriculum.

I could not get my head around the notion that I was expected to demand that all my teachers taught a rigid curriculum designed for mainstream pupils. These severely disabled children were being expected to learn French, geography, history (it was the Romans that term) and maths to name but a few. I saw in that moment how all the individual developmental education that we had worked so hard for, to enable the children to learn, would be pushed aside and the arguments against putting our children in 'normal' schools would be gone.

I guessed that parents would be impressed, believing that their children, through learning 'proper' subjects, would be 'normal' just like every other child. I often had difficulty in explaining to a parent why their child was in a class with children who appeared to them to be more disabled. I could envisage the same responses from parents of children in mainstream schools when they found a severely disabled child in their child's class.

A few days later, I had a frustrating interview with a member of staff whose job it was to accompany children on a taxi to and from home. Teachers in the nursery came to tell me that this woman had arrived at school very much the worse for wear from alcohol. By the time I went to find her, she had disappeared. So, with all my other burdens, I had to step in and escort the child home.

I saw the woman next day and confronted her. She objected and was very rude when I said she could not be responsible for children if she was drinking alcohol. She went home and claimed constructive dismissal. There followed a full-scale official inquiry, which took up many hours in writing reports, and interviewing parents and staff who had witnessed the problem. The child's mother waded in with complaints about our lack of care for her child; she suggested the escort had smelled of alcohol frequently and staggered about. It was exhausting and took me away from the many tasks I had to do.

A meeting was called by the education officer, with union representatives for the employee present. At that time, the ruling political party in our area was very left-wing Labour. The education officers were wary of raising any issues that the Labour members might see as discriminatory, and so issues like mine were hushed up and the union member placated.

The outcome of the meeting produced a reprimand for me for being 'hard' on an employee. She was reinstated and belligerent toward me. She tried to gather a petition to have me removed from my post, but was not successful. Nobody was happy with this outcome. The teachers and parents said I had let them down.

Thankfully, there were few of these unpleasant disputes to deal with, but they left their mark, since I tried to be reasonable and fair always. I learned the hard way that managing people is a dog's breakfast.

———❧———

On the plus side, there were many, many heroic staff who would go the extra mile for me and for the children without being asked – one even taking a child home overnight because the parents were not at home at the end of the day. Another fostered a child when the family had broken up. Their understanding of my principles and values regarding children was a great comfort to me in difficult times.

CHAPTER TWENTY-SEVEN

Breakdown

THE INCIDENT REGARDING A DRUNKEN MEMBER OF THE staff was the last straw for me. It came at a moment when I was severely stressed and feeling very alone in the pressures that faced me. At the same time, my marriage to Patrick was suffering because I was distracted continually by my workload and I had a lack of time for our common interests outside work. I made some disastrous mistakes, and – in the end, after long discussions – we agreed to part. The pressure of my work had led to this, and I blame myself for not paying enough attention to my family. It was a terrible time for everyone, but particularly for our children.

By the early months of 1989, my health had begun to suffer; in due course, I had a hysterectomy, followed by a period of time at home to rest and recuperate.

My husband moved out of our home in January 1989 to be with his new partner, and we put the house on the market. With hindsight, this was a hasty decision. Our beloved home, called Brincliffe, where our children had enjoyed so much fun, had given me a security I had never known before. I felt it would not be possible for us to go on living there as a broken family.

The children stayed with me. Our arrangements were shared very amicably, and we were all able to stay living within a few miles of each other, so David got to see his dad as much as he saw me.

The rift that had grown between my husband and Shaun, his adopted son, was never healed. It was far from an ideal situation, and one I still feel sad about.

My sense of failure at another marriage breakdown was intense, though I talked to no one about it and know now that I should have sought help. I began to see how difficult it must have been for my husband to get close to me when my head was always full of school issues. We never rowed – though there were lots of long silent spells – so the children never had to experience rows and tantrums, but it must have been a time of great anxiety for them. To their great credit, they have never rebuked me for those difficult times, and I love them dearly for their bravery and forgiveness.

In February 1988, I had enrolled on a week's residential course in management for headteachers and senior officers of the education department. I arrived at the conference house one Monday morning, wondering what to expect. After an introduction to the course, we were all assigned to small groups. The group I joined consisted of five men and me. There should have been another woman, but she was ill. We were given tasks to do to enable us to assimilate the principles of working in teams to get jobs done more efficiently.

By the second session, I had got the measure of the other members of the group, who talked incessantly with no regard for me at all. I could not get a word in. Eventually, I banged on the table and said, "Now look, you men, I'm here and I have a right to give my views. I am not going to sit here all week looking meek."

There was a bit of a silence, and then we continued, with my views being sought almost too much as a result. However, from then on, we had a great time, and achieved some very important practices and principles for our different working roles.

At the end of the week, one of the staff from the company Coverdale came to me and said, "Anita, we've been watching you all week."

Oh help, I thought. *I've been too outspoken.*

He went on to say that the company were selecting suitable candidates to take on a training role, and they would like to offer this opportunity to me.

I nearly fell off my chair.

There was more than a little envy from the men around.

Amongst the delegates in our group was John. He had developed a great fascination for me, which I was totally unaware of. At the end of the course when we were required to give written feedback about each member of our group, he could not find anything negative to say about me!

When I returned to my school on the Monday, he appeared after lunch and declared, "I was just passing and thought I would pop in to see your school."

His job at the time was as county adviser to secondary schools across Derbyshire, and our paths would not cross normally. He was very keen to see me and asked me to meet him for a drink.

We went through a difficult period subsequently, culminating with him moving in with me in 1990.

As I write this, John and I have been married for over twenty years and are very happy. His personality suits me best. We are interested in the same things, have had many adventures, run a successful business together and have travelled widely.

I became a part-time trainer for the Coverdale organisation, helping to lead groups of headteachers and senior administrators in managing teamwork more effectively. I fitted all this in with all my other responsibilities – it was madness. I was able to take away an excellent system for working with groups of colleagues to good effect. Inevitably, I was piling yet more work on myself.

I struggled on in my job until May 2003. One Sunday evening whilst ironing, I collapsed in tears and could not stop weeping. John tried to help me by getting me to identify all the tasks I was dreading facing in the next week and prioritising for me. It was useless; I could barely understand what he was saying and felt extreme panic. I lay awake all night, and the one thought in my head was that I could not continue – I could not go back into the school. By the next morning, I had resolved to see my GP.

He took one look at my red, tearful face and said, "What in heaven's name is this government doing to you teachers? My surgery is full of distraught, overworked teachers. Right, you are to stay at home and get well again, and think carefully about the future."

I felt so grateful to him for understanding the situation, and he supported me through a period of sick leave until I could make a rational decision about my future. For two years, I had panic attacks when I thought of going back into the school building. I went to see the local education officer, who expressed some surprise that I had felt unsupported through all the changes that were going on in education at that time.

I continued to feel very guilty and angry that I could not continue in my job. I did not know where to turn for help. Ultimately, I thought of a colleague in the advisory service who worked with John and with whom I had worked on the Coverdale training, and John asked him to meet us. He came to our home and, amidst my tears, he began to help me to think differently about my situation.

He said to me, "Now, what do you want to do with the rest of your working life?"

I replied with the sort of statement that I have heard so many times over the years since, from people in crisis, "I've no idea. I've only ever been a teacher."

"Anita, I want you to write down all those aspects of your career that you are proud of."

This was tricky to start with. With his encouragement, I produced a long list of positive outcomes from the work of the school and in my private life.

He studied my list for some time, then announced, "This is an impressive list of the skills and personal qualities you have gained over the years. There are many directions you could take in your life."

He produced a very long list of ideas about the kinds of work I could do using these skills, including self-employment. The idea of being self-employed seemed laughable to me at that moment. I could never have imagined the direction my life would take next, nor perceive the exciting discoveries ahead of me.

Before all that, something amazing happened.

CHAPTER TWENTY-EIGHT

That's My Dad

MY NIECE DAWN RANG ME ONE DAY EARLY IN 2006. SHE declared, "Aunty Anita, I have some news for you. Are you sitting down?"

"Why?" I enquired.

"I have found out about your dad, my grandfather."

"How? What!"

"I went onto a website called Genes Reunited and typed in his name as a query. A reply came back immediately. Your dad remarried and had another family. You have three half-brothers and a sister. I have sent an email to and had a reply from Elaine, your half-sister, who has been searching for her father's children. She would like to contact you."

I was stunned. I had given up any idea of finding my dad. Now, here was an opportunity to know him.

"I'm sorry, your dad is not alive. He died in 1996," Dawn said.

It took me a few days to pluck up courage to contact Elaine. I sent her a brief email, and she replied. She told me that my dad had always talked about my sister and me. Elaine had said she wanted a sister badly, and Dad had said that he had two little girls somewhere, but he did not know where they were. She offered to send me a photo of him.

Dawn continued her research using the website and, consequently, got in touch with several of Dad's nieces – our cousins.

That spring, after several happy holidays in the Algarve, John and I purchased an apartment in Vilamoura. We spent time there whenever our busy work schedules allowed. Family and friends came to spend holidays with us, and we had some great times. We grew to love the Portuguese, who are kind, hospitable and like British people.

In March the same year, Jane – David's former nanny – came to spend time with us whilst recovering from surgery. I told her about our recent news and she asked me to show her how to log on to the website.

Immediately, I saw a message from Elaine. It said, "Dad's photo."

"Oh, Anita. Are you ready for this?" Jane asked.

"Let's have a coffee first!" I replied.

Now, when I was a small child, one regular face on the television was that of the comedian Arthur Askey. He was short, and had big, dark-framed glasses and a cheeky smile. Whenever I saw him on the screen, I would cry, run out of the room and be terribly upset. I opened the photo file and the face of my dad was very similar to that of Arthur Askey. He had large, dark-framed glasses and a cheeky smile. For all the intervening years I had forgotten his face, but now it was familiar and a little unnerving.

Elaine and I exchanged more emails and spoke on the phone. Finally, we arranged to meet at our house. It was a beautiful, warm July afternoon when all our children and their partners gathered around the table in the garden, with the champagne ready, waiting to meet Elaine and Mick.

They arrived, we hugged, and she said, "Dad would be over the moon that we have found you."

It was a very happy occasion, with lots of shared photographs and champagne!

Mick, looking round at all our family, asserted, "I can see your dad and his family in each face around the table."

Later, we travelled down to Berkhamstead, where Elaine and Mick lived, to meet the rest of my half-siblings and their children.

As we sat, a group of strangers weirdly connected to me, one brother said, "It's really strange to hear you speak about my dad."

"He was my dad first," I said.

That was perhaps not kind, but it was the only time I felt resentment toward this new family. Since then, we have become closer in the way that grown-up brothers and sisters should be, and we have shared holidays, weddings and time together.

⁂

John and I visited my dad's grave. I shed tears for all that might have been and all that was lost to me, forever.

On his gravestone was a treble clef, remembering his love of music. Below was written these words: "To live in the hearts of those you love is not to die." What a fitting epitaph.

Part Three

SUPPORT INTO WORK (SIW)

Go with the people.
Live with them.
Learn from them.
Love them.
Start with what they know.
Build with what they have.
But with the best leaders,
When the work is done,
The task accomplished,
The people will say, "We have done this ourselves."

(Ancient Taoist Poem)

CHAPTER TWENTY-NINE

Inspiring Others to Achieve Their Dreams

WHEN I RETIRED FROM MY JOB AS HEADTEACHER AT A special school on the grounds of ill health, I took some time to rest, recover and get my energy back. During the following autumn and winter, I had three separate flu-like illnesses, which left me feeling totally exhausted, with a lot of pain around my joints and with mild depression. I was unable to do very much – even making a bed would leave me exhausted. I went to my doctor and, in due course, was referred to a rheumatologist, who – after looking at my list of strange symptoms – declared, "You have fibromyalgia."

I knew nothing about this condition and was alarmed to be told that there was no cure for my chronic fatigue and the pains in all my muscles. I was prescribed anti-inflammatory drugs, and told to take it easy and to avoid stress. After reading what information I could get hold of – which was very little at that time – and hearing my GP say that this chronic condition was a new fad, I was lost to know how to go forward. The symptoms were, and still are, very much influenced by stress and I had had plenty of that in my life.

Since those early years, I have learned a lot about fibromyalgia and have met several people suffering from it. It is always comforting, in a strange way, to hear others talk about similar random symptoms – it confirms my belief that the condition is widespread and not just in my head. It is now accepted by doctors as a recognised disability and many more strategies for managing the pain are available. The irony for me is that it is now classed as a disability; this after all my years working with disabled young people!

———⦿———

At the beginning of 1994, I visited an old colleague, Dawn, who had been a teacher at the school where I was the headteacher. Dawn had moved on and was then employed as a support teacher at the local college of further education, working with young adults with learning difficulties. During her years as a teacher, I was continually amazed and impressed at the way she could motivate and inspire disabled children to help them to become more independent.

Over a cup of coffee, she asked me, "What are you going to do with the rest of your life?"

I said I didn't know, but I certainly did not want to return to teaching, which had given me so much stress in recent years. She, like all my family and friends, knew me as a very busy, active person; I, in contrast, could not imagine how I could ever work again, feeling as ill as I did every day.

She thought for a while then ventured, "You know, these disabled young people I am working with at the college want what other students want – to find a job, get some money, fall in love and get married. There is nobody out in the wider community to help them get work experience and find a job. When I worked at St Andrew's School with you, I remember how we found work experience for the teenagers in places such as local shops, stacking shelves; in a library; or in a car wash. Someone with your knowledge could help these young people achieve their dreams."

I listened very hard and began to think.

Returning home I told my husband John about my visit and Dawn's comments. "I think I could do that," I said with some enthusiasm. Fate had taken a hand again.

I felt that if I could get involved with the students as they left college, I might be able to help them find work experience and, hopefully, jobs, with me working on a gentle part-time basis at my own pace. John was delighted at my enthusiasm and encouraged me to explore the possibilities.

Dawn had given me the number of an organisation in Salford doing similar work with disabled people, and so, a few days later, I made an appointment to go and visit them. The organisation was funded by the local authority and was having some success in placing people with learning difficulties in local companies – initially, on a work-experience basis. They admitted they had a long way to go in learning how to match jobs accurately to the young people's limited skills. The manager was very helpful and gave me the name of another organisation to visit. My first venture into the world of networking had begun.

At that juncture, I had no idea how this would all work out, but decided to take one step at a time. As I have already mentioned in Chapter 27, an old friend of ours had sat with me one day at home after I retired from my school job, and he made me focus on the successes of my career and my life experiences to date, in order to lift me out of the depression I was experiencing and to help me see ways forward. This exercise was very helpful because, like many people who have needed to make a big change in their lives, I was tempted to dwell on the failures. It was a very emotional process and hard to carry out. He encouraged me to list the skills I had gained throughout all of my life and work experiences, and then we began to analyse the possible work directions those skills could lead to. Amongst them was the possibility of being self-employed.

That's ridiculous, I thought, *I have great trouble with managing my own budget never mind running a business!* Out loud, I said a phrase that I was to hear again and again from clients, with slightly different words, in the years to come, "But I have only ever been a teacher." I had to confess that the skills list was considerable and helped me gain the courage to move forward and to look at new possibilities.

Our friend had, inadvertently, given me a valuable tool to use with clients trying to find a new direction in life. Seeking help and support from people they knew, asking those people to get involved in the job seeker's quest to find a new career and identifying their skills – that was to become a sound method for me as I visited organisations and gained insights and introductions to others who might help me achieve my goal.

Finally, a chance conversation with a neighbour who worked for the Chamber of Commerce in Derby gave me a way forward. I enrolled on a business start-up course and learned the rudiments of business plans, bookkeeping, employment law and, most importantly, marketing. The course tutor grilled us about our business ideas and their marketability – or lack thereof. He did not know what to make of mine. I thought it stood as good a chance as the young woman planning to run a dog-grooming business, getting customers by walking her dog in a local park.

I did need to be earning to replace some of the income I had lost through early retirement from education, and so, at my neighbour's suggestion, I telephoned an officer at the local Training and Enterprise Council (TEC) and asked if I could air my business ideas with him. I must have made a good impression because I was offered a small contract to find employment for twelve disabled people within a year, with free accommodation in a building in the city centre, alongside advisers for hearing and visually impaired students.

In the spring of 1995, I began my new career.

CHAPTER THIRTY

Help Needed

AN UNSEEN CONSEQUENCE OF BEING IN THIS OFFICE BEGAN to emerge quickly. Whilst I was making contacts through Dawn with ex-students (whom I had known throughout their school careers), messages from members of the public needing help with all manner of disabilities began to appear on my desk. The two advisers already in the office could only help those with specific impairments. I was to become the conduit for helping all the rest.

Within weeks, I was inundated and had over fifty people on my books. In those days, there was far less known about the abilities and employment potential of people born with lifelong and multiple impairments, as well as those who had acquired disabilities during their lifetime. Gaining employment or changing direction in work was very hard for them, as was finding appropriate help about what kind of jobs they could do. All of these people were desperate to succeed in getting a job.

I knew nothing about the world of adult training and contracting, so I had to find a way to proceed with my new role from the perspective of my years in education, my training in counselling skills, and my firm belief that disabled people deserved help to enable them to succeed and compete with others in the workplace. I started talking to and exploring possibilities with each new client to form a holistic assessment of their capabilities, skills and barriers to finding employment. I knew that employers would have to take account of the applicants' personal baggage and physical limitations, just as I had to do for myself when starting up this new career.

As a business venture, it was never going to make me rich, but working with disadvantaged people gave me tremendous job satisfaction and the joy of seeing some people achieve excellent new careers. I began by believing I could work part-time and thus cope with the limitations of my disability. As the months went by, I was in danger of being overwhelmed, with many people seeking my help and with multiple issues to take account of in their lives, and so – after much discussion at home – my husband agreed to work with me part-time.

The workload expanded quickly to fill our time and we were both working together full-time by the beginning of 1996. We were offering computer training and a 'preparation for work' course, which we developed to prepare disabled people for applying for jobs. We began to receive some funding to do this, and employed two advisers with much experience in training adults. We had to increase this number month by month as we became more effective. There was much to learn in a short space of time, as we had our first introduction to the rules and regulations of the employment service.

I was often very tired and had to lie down for a nap in my car in the car park at lunchtime because of fatigue. It was this overwhelming lack of energy that gave me the most problems day by day. I was not good at working at a slower pace, but I enjoyed the job immensely.

―❦―

One of my first clients, T, a man in his early thirties with Down's syndrome, was referred to me by an adviser from the local employment-service office. One of their disability employment advisers had T on her list and had found him a job, but was unable to give him the level of support in the workplace that he needed to have a chance of success. She asked if I could help him, and I agreed.

I met T and was delighted to get to know him. He spoke in a very quiet, respectful way. He could read newspapers and get about town independently, and he lived with his elderly Italian mother. He was very excited about starting work at a factory making balloons, on the outskirts of the city. I visited the company with him and explained carefully to the employer what sort of help he might need and offered my services at any time if he or they experienced any difficulties. I arranged with T that he should meet me just before 7.30am on the day he was due to start to learn how to clock in and wished him good luck.

Arriving in good time on his first morning, I found T already in the building; not wanting to be late, he had clocked in at 6.30am! I had difficulty in explaining that he should clock in at the correct time. He assured me he didn't mind starting earlier, even though nobody else was there. I began to gain an idea of the range of other social skills that such clients needed to acquire in order to function in the workplace.

Party balloons were manufactured at the factory, and T was placed in the packing area with several skilled employees. Completed balloons passed along the line to the packers, who inspected each one for defects then dropped each into one of a series of trays moving past on a conveyor belt. At the end of the line, each tray of balloons in various colours, shapes and sizes was tipped automatically into a plastic bag, which was sealed immediately and dropped into a cardboard box ready for dispatch to the retailer. There was no margin for error!

T's job, initially, was to sort balloons of two different colours and shapes into plastic trays as they passed by him. The workers were extremely helpful after I explained that they would initially need to break down the component parts of the task into simple stages, so that he could get a thorough grasp of the job and get up to speed. (And so that he could learn not to talk at the same time because he might miss some). I sat alongside him whilst he learned to put one colour at a time into each tray, then I left him happy at his task, with a huge smile on his face.

"Ring me if there's a problem," I said to the supervisor as I left.

All went well for a few days and then the phone rang. It was the supervisor, who said, "Can you come in? T has a problem."

I agreed, and soon set off to go to the factory.

When I arrived, I asked, "What's the matter?"

"Well, you see, Anita, they're going too fast."

T had been given an additional task, which was to examine each balloon for faults around its neck. True to his meticulous nature, he was spending a lot of time examining each balloon carefully, whilst the trays rolled by and balloons fell into a bag and were sealed, without the contracted number of twelve to a bag. Over time and with very supportive colleagues, T became more proficient, but he could never reach the necessary speed to fulfil the job.

"And, anyway," he said to me one day, "I'm colour blind!"

It was another salutary lesson for me to learn about knowing in advance a client's skill set.

During one of my monitoring visits, the office staff asked if T had a bank account into which they could pay his wages. I was sure he had none, but agreed to talk to his mother.

Arriving at his house, I discovered that his mother spoke little English. She was quick to thank me for helping him, and I tried to explain that he needed to open an account for his wages. I suggested a building society account, so he could more easily draw out money.

She responded with, "Please, no cheque cards!"

How wise.

I took him to a building society, where he encountered a major obstacle: he had no documents to prove his status – no utility bills, no passport and no National Insurance (NI) number. Eventually, we got it sorted, I deposited £10 in the account for him and we left the building with T clutching his passbook. I stressed to him that he must keep it safe, so that no one could steal his money.

He patted his jacket pocket and looked knowingly at me. "There's just one thing, Anita," he said. "I've never paid tax and National Insurance before... now I can!"

Whilst driving him home, my husband asked him if anyone else lived at his house besides his mother.

"Only my brother," T said.

"Is he older than you or younger?" my husband enquired.

"The same, of course," T replied. "He's my twin. He's got a job in computers."

In the end, T decided that the conveyor belt was not for him. The employer was very accommodating and provided other tasks, but in the end T left. He was not deterred and was keen to find more work. We were able to place him in a number of jobs over the next ten years. He got temporary work in supermarkets, stacking shelves, and in the warehouse of a publishing company. Without exception, he got on well with everyone at work. He was fully independent, both walking and on public transport, and still has a lovely smile when we see him out and about. During the years we knew him, he was seldom out of work.

T is a perfect example of matching work to the abilities of a severely disabled man. He also illustrates the difficulties faced in matching skills closely to the needs of the busy workplace, to the levels of support in the workplace that clients may need and to the job satisfaction when we got it right.

CHAPTER THIRTY-ONE

Taking Care
of the People

OUR GROWING REPUTATION FOR HELPING ANY DISABLED person led the TEC to increase our funding in order to provide further training to prepare clients for work. Job clubs were not a new concept in the training field, but we had to develop a programme that could help our disadvantaged clients identify their skills and barriers in order to prepare for job interviews. In addition, they needed to understand the climate and responsibilities in the workplace, if they had never worked.

For clients who had to change career direction because of a disabling condition the demands were similar. Every person arrived with lots of personal baggage. Addressing those individual issues was our major challenge. We did not follow the usual training practice of placing a client immediately with one of a few employers known to that company. We needed to seek a suitable employer for each client's needs. The range of need was enormous.

In employing others to work with us, we stressed our need for a complementary team that, above anything else, had the needs of each client at the centre of their work. In 1996, this came as a welcome surprise to advisers who had worked in large companies where income for the company was the driving force. I once heard a motivational trainer opine, "Take care of the clients and the business will come." This was certainly true in terms of numbers and successes for us.

What should we call our company? At the start, we discussed what we should be called around the table at home. We felt that we needed to stress our supportive role in helping clients gain employment. David, my youngest son, has excellent drawing skills and he produced a diagram of a hand holding the initials SIW, which stands for Support Into Work; this seemed perfect. We were later persuaded that a publishing agency might design a new and better logo. They charged us thousands of pounds, but could not come up with anything more eye-catching and appropriate. Our company became widely known as SIW.

Having agreed to put on a training course that would last for two weeks, we needed to agree on content for the ten-day, thirty-hours-a-week programme. Our new advisers had sound experience in running such a programme, known as a job club, but not with the client group we had, and not full-time.

It was already apparent that, in the traditional model, clients were expected to spend several hours searching newspapers for job adverts with minimum help. Many had very poor reading and writing skills. Some could not read at all. Many had suffered bad experiences in their school years, which had prevented them from learning vital skills. One man in his late twenties described being made to kneel in a box lined with pencils throughout the lesson because he could not read what was written on the board. Another was locked in a cupboard if he gave a wrong answer. It was easy to see how some young people are switched off from learning in such a hostile environment. We all felt outrage that this should be happening in our local schools in the twenty-first century. I had personal sympathy with the horrors of what was written on the blackboard from my childhood. Others spoke of the shame they felt in their families where children could read and write, but they could not.

Increasingly, the modern workplace requires the ability to read and use a computer. In addition, some clients' short attention span for formal activities such as researching jobs meant that a different activities were needed. We asked our clients, "What would you love to have a go at?" Answers came thick and fast: drawing, computing, gardening, painting, singing, helping with children and many, many more. When broken down into smaller, manageable activities, it became possible gradually to give them some of those activities, which helped develop their confidence and social skills.

We would sometimes hold sessions on such important topics as 'Why do we have rules at work?', 'Who makes the rules?', 'What does the law say employers have to do for you?', 'What are your responsibilities in the workplace?' and 'What do you know about keeping safe in the workplace?' Each subject created a good discussion for learning, without the need for them to read all about it initially. It also identified the common issues in all jobs.

CHAPTER THIRTY-TWO

The Women's Group and a Support Group for Men

IT WAS SOON NOTICEABLE THAT MANY OF THE WOMEN WHO came to us welcomed the opportunity to talk on a one-to-one about their lives and their fears. We needed to manage this in a way that made the most of the time available, and the Women's Group was established. I ran this group once a week.

I had some counselling training, which came in handy for facilitating conversations. In practice, I usually just had to 'throw a pebble in the pond' and they were off! 'How to be assertive in the workplace' was a popular topic. Coping with male put-downs at work – and at home – was another. Clients found a common bond in hearing from others with the same problems and in learning about how they had resolved them.

Sometimes we would invite an outside speaker to the group, at their request. A female vicar who had once been a dinner lady and a local female Member of Parliament (MP) each talked to the group about their lives, successes and difficulties in being a woman at work. They were entertaining and spoke of simple strategies to use to move forward to reach one's goals in life.

These group sessions diversified into weekly painting and drawing classes, crafts, embellishing clothing, etc. We made visits to the Mayoress's Parlour and enjoyed a look behind the scenes at the local theatre. Tickets for productions were donated, and some of the women were able to see a live production for the very first time.

The women were asked for feedback about how the group had helped them; this is what they said: "There is more sympathy, empathy and understanding in a group which has only women members"; "It's good to talk with others who have the same issues"; "I am gaining confidence; I feel good and know I can get a job"; "My health issues are understood"; "You can let your feelings out"; "It feels like we are being stroked!"; "It's a safe environment"; and "The group decided the programme of activities with some guidance on what would be feasible. We have sessions on identifying skills and personal qualities, handling stress, relaxation techniques and make-up for interviews, to name but a few."

The company also introduced classes in painting and drawing, and making clothes. One woman wrote to me, saying this:

I came to Support Into Work because I wanted to learn. I didn't know what to expect. But I am learning to read and spell and manage my money. I wish the days were longer so I could learn more.

My confidence has grown by coming to the Women's Group, realising that I am not the only person experiencing difficulties, and with the help of the group I have found the way to deal with them. Shadowing J our receptionist helped me realise I had skills to offer to an employer I never thought I had.

C, a member of our staff, had this message about M, a client:

She has changed the way I think about disabled people. M being at SIW makes a difference – to the way clients respond in their group work and in the way we do our job. She, without knowing it, demands respect and sets standards that enrich all our lives.

One day my husband said to me, "I am being asked why there is no Men's Group."

I had no immediate answer except to think that we had no advisers who had the time or talent to deliver this kind of training. However, we recognised the genuine need for this, and my husband John and I started a group together.

The groups were voluntary. The men were nervous, scornful and keen in equal measure. Initially, some opted out, but most decided to join in after hearing what happened in the sessions.

One client, A, who came had a severe back problem sustained from an injury at work. He needed to lie on the floor from time to time to get some relief from the pain. He had difficulty in looking forward to being fit enough to get back into work and had no ideas about what he might do. Another client had memory loss, and was determined that no work other than the engineering job he had lost through his mental illness would interest him. Yet another man had been invalided out of the army, as he was confined to a wheelchair after a horrific experience in Iraq. Subsequently, two out of the three moved into full-time employment in a new sphere from their previous work. Sadly, we could not help the man with mental health issues, since we could not persuade him to focus on a new direction.

We were sceptical at first about whether the men would want to talk openly about their experiences. We found that by posing significant questions – such as "What do you enjoy doing?", "Do you have a hobby?" and "How do you spend your day?" – we could set the ball rolling and sit back. Conversation always flowed, and they were frank with each other and mostly very supportive. They warmed to the notion that they were not alone in their situation and could identify with others going through similar experiences. Many had answers that others may not have thought of. It was a great learning experience for John and me.

The individual help that some people needed outside of these sessions was more easily identified, and we could refer them to the most appropriate person. Some of the men began to volunteer within the company's training sessions to support vulnerable clients logging on to a computer, reading instructions or speaking up in training groups. This volunteer programme became a valuable asset to our work over many years and was of interest to the employment service and other training organisations – including trainee police cadets. We made links with the local volunteering service and were able to help clients move into other activities in and around the city.

The man with the severe back pain spent some time at our centre helping other clients and becoming a bit more mobile. He appreciated being able to lie down whenever the pain in his back was too much. In exploring his hobbies, we discovered that he was interested in amateur radio and was spending some time each week at the local hospital playing requests from patients over the hospital system. In time, when he was more mobile, we approached the local radio station with him to seek a work-experience placement. They took him on and, on realising his talents gradually, gave him projects to develop. Sadly, at that time there was no vacancy for him to join as an employee. He found an advertisement in the local press for a development worker to start up a project in a poor area of the city to teach young people about radio broadcasting. He got the job and was very successful in promoting the project around the city, gaining extra funding and a reputation for his skills with the youngsters. As this project came to an end after three years, he moved back to the local radio station to a full-time job as a presenter. His name is known all over the city and he has his own programme every morning.

My husband's role involved seeking funding to be able to carry out all the extra activities that our clients gained so much from. He had to search for funding streams, which would fit around people's needs – especially those who could only manage a few hours a week initially. State funding did not allow for any variation from the regulations for all clients, even though ours needed a much longer time to be prepared for work. This was always stressful and complicated when clients joined a group that was funded in a different way. Red tape, as ever, often got in the way of doing the best thing for individuals, and there was no way we could explain or justify that to our clients. We seldom had to turn anyone away.

CHAPTER THIRTY-THREE

Changing Lives — Unusual Work Experiences

JOHN WAS VISITING A DAY NURSERY ONE DAY WITH A VIEW to placing a client there for work experience. There he met the organiser, Maggie; she was a wonderful, kind, caring woman who was experiencing extreme harassment in her job from a woman at the local council. John asked me to go to see her at home, as she had gone on sick leave. She needed someone to talk to. I found her lying on a couch, utterly dejected and at rock bottom about the accusations being made against her. I visited Maggie several times over the following few weeks, talking through the issues, helping her to get her energy back and doing the work of identifying her potential, as I had experienced in the past from a friend. I suggested that, because of her experience of working with departments of the city council, she might like to come to our training centre to be a volunteer helper. She proved to be worth her weight in gold and thus began a long and happy relationship with us.

Initially, she helped in classes, but we employed her full-time eventually, and she took over the initial assessment process from me as I began a training programme for young people. Because of her wealth of experience in the city, she was known by lots of organisations and was soon able to identify the exact person for a client to ring to get help with benefits, housing issues, child care and many more issues. In addition, she trained to become one of our assessors for National Vocational Qualifications (NVQs) and was particularly good at working with and motivating teenagers.

She never could get her head around computing, but asked for a computer on her desk, like all the other advisers. One day, when she was out of the centre, as a prank, our information technology (IT) technician put a monitor and keyboard on her desk – but no processor!

When she came back into the office, she saw the monitor and squealed with delight. "Oh! Just what I wanted! Thank you so much!" she exclaimed. She sat at her desk, tapped at the keyboard and said in her broad Scottish dialect, "It didnae work for me!"

She stayed with the company for many years and became a firm friend – everybody liked her. She could converse easily with both younger and older clients, and always showed her care and concern for each of them. Ultimately, she retired through bad health, and she wrote this to John and me when she left:

> I wish to put on record the way you have assisted me to recover my life over the last seven years, identifying how supportive you have been throughout this period. I had a severe nervous breakdown in 1997–98 arising from ill treatment at work and resulting in a prolonged court case. While the final outcome was a success, my personal circumstances had reached rock bottom. I had become incapable of doing anything for myself; I had lost the will to live, attempting suicide on a number of occasions.
>
> I was approached by John Elwell at the worst time of my crises and persuaded that I could help them with their business. I joined as a volunteer at first then went through their Preparation for Work Programme with the company. John advised me to talk to Anita, his wife and business partner.

Anita visited me at home on several occasions, where I was unable to move off the sofa, so depressed had I become. Over several months she gave me extensive counselling and things gradually started to come together for me – I began to see once again that I could have a life worth living. Things started to look more positive. The continued support and guidance I had received was so deep and valuable that a lasting personal relationship has developed that I know will last me throughout my life. I cannot emphasize too strongly that both John and Anita have been supportive throughout this period, and were solely responsible for assisting me to get back into life. Looking back now, I know that their interventions were designed to try and help me progress my life once again and take charge. This is how they work with everybody.

I have now been employed in the company for six years and have experienced at first hand how clients are supported, including those with health problems and disabilities. From my heart I truly see this work as unique within Derby; the first thought is always in the client's interests. It is absolutely the case that this work has transformed the lives of many clients – for the better, and whose journey we continue to watch with great pride and joy.

Yours sincerely...

This unsolicited testimony and many others from satisfied clients gave me the joy and motivation to believe I had found, almost by chance, another great career. I still have all those letters to remind me on a sad day how far I have come in my life.

H was a young client with a big voice to match his personality. He could talk for England, and did! He had learning disabilities, was looked after by his elderly Afro-Caribbean mother, and had impeccable manners, a winning smile and an infectious laugh. I first heard him being interviewed by my husband in an adjoining room.

He stated, "My mother says I talk too much, Mr Elwell. Do you think I talk too much, Mr Elwell? I don't think so myself; what do you think?" And on and on he went…

An opportunity arose for someone to work in a smart hotel kitchen on the edge of town. It was decided by the SIW team that this might be suitable for H, and, as often happens, the hotel chef had a relative with a learning disability, so he was sympathetic to the idea and willing to give H a go.

One morning John arrived at the hotel with H at the appointed time. He was spruced up as if for a wedding and very excited. They sat in the hotel atrium, and were served with coffee and biscuits in grand style.

H looked about him and began, "This is a wonderful hotel, Mr Elwell. I really like it. Are these biscuits for me? I would like to work in this hotel, Mr Elwell; it's a really smart place. I think this is the job for me."

My husband had to caution him not to talk his way out of an opportunity!

After meeting the head chef, H was shown around the kitchen and offered a trial work placement for a few weeks. Our commitment was to be on call and to go to the hotel at any time if there were problems.

H got on well at first. The staff in the kitchen were all very supportive and helpful. His job was to load and unload the trays of crockery from the large commercial dishwasher. Time passed and all was quiet from H and the hotel.

In due course, a call came into SIW, saying "We have a problem."

On visiting H, John found that the pace of the crockery coming out of the dishwasher was too quick for him. H, being the sociable man he was, was too busy chatting to concentrate on the job in hand, and plates were flying everywhere. He had to leave.

It could have been viewed as a disaster for H; however, he gained valuable experience in a real workplace and new information to add to his curriculum vitae (CV), which was a bit thin on job experience. He was soon up for a new opportunity and forgot his desire to work in a hotel.

Morrisons supermarket provided his next work-experience placement. The human resources (HR) manager was very sympathetic and gave him some training in managing the trolleys in the car park. It was stressed to H that he must not try to steer more than a certain number of trolleys at one time for safety reasons. Again, all went well for a while.

One day, H forgot the rule and decided he could manage to push a larger number of trolleys to save time. He steered them straight into the parked car of a customer. Some damage was done, but H made it far worse by saying to the customer, "Your car was in my way!"

The HR manager called us in. H got a gentle telling off and was told, "Remember, the customer is always right. Morrisons has to pay for the damage to customers' cars."

H was very contrite and was given another chance.

Time passed until, one day, the phone rang again. We were asked if we could call into Morrisons as there had been an incident. H had again collided his trolleys with a customer's car, but – on remembering that the customer is always right – he had declared quickly, "Don't worry, sir, it wasn't your fault; Morrisons will pay!"

That was the end of that job. To her credit, the HR manager persevered and gave him tasks to do under the supervision of other staff. He enjoyed clearing tables in the restaurant and chatting to customers, but, being H, he talked too much, forgot about the task in hand frequently and, again, the crockery piled up.

His final attempt at training for work was at a small supermarket near his home, stacking shelves, which he managed to keep.

J was a young man with learning difficulties sent to us by the jobcentre because other training companies could not manage his behaviour.

G was a middle-aged man with learning difficulties and poor understanding of instructions. He could not read or write, but wanted a job working with cars. John found him an opportunity to wash cars with a small company in the city. He learned the job quite quickly, but we were called to the company on one hot summer's day. John arrived to find G stretched out on the tarmac in the middle of the car park.

"What are you doing down there, G?" asked John.

"Sunbathing – it's too hot to work!" was his reply.

The manager said ruefully, "I wouldn't mind, but he won't move to let the cars manoeuvre round him!"

When I was a headteacher with responsibility for the education of disabled children, I had always had a strong belief in the importance of teaching the pupils to learn basic social skills to help them become as independent as possible. Coping in the many and complex everyday situations that we find around us has proved to be just as important for adults with disabilities trying to find their way in the busy modern workplace.

One major impediment to work for people with learning disabilities is the issue of state benefits. I was soon to discover that finding a job for these clients was often in conflict with the benefits money paid to them but managed by their relative on their behalf. This money was often a considerable sum, since it was assumed that people with learning disabilities were unemployable.

I remember visiting the sister of one client to talk about his offer of a job. I was elated about this outcome, but she was not.

"What you have got to remember," she said to me, "is that his money goes to pay our rent. We can't manage without it. So if you put him in this job, we will lose our money."

This came as a shock to me, since I had assumed that benefits were used for the care and needs of the individual, which would be replaced by income when he was in work. This issue became highlighted nationally when disability charities began to recognise this barrier for people.

The government responded with the stock reply, "The benefits are clearly intended for the individual."

Over the years, SIW had many clients with mental health issues who were referred to us by the jobcentres. The advisers there got to know that we were willing to see and try to help such people. Sometimes, we simply improved their confidence and helped them to come to terms with their limitations, which led to new aims for realistic employment. It seemed valuable and worthwhile work to us, though placing such clients in work was often very difficult.

There is still a huge stigma attached to people with mental health conditions in the workplace, and it takes a very special employer to be able to develop that person's skills at their own pace, whilst protecting the need of the business to make a profit. Many of our clients needed daily support in working through the demands of the workplace – and building relationships with other employees. This approach is expensive and time consuming, but very worthwhile and the right thing to do for our workforce.

One difficult issue that came up in training sessions was when to tell an employer about a disabling condition. Some of our clients had bad experiences of talking about their disability at an interview and being turned down because of their issues. Many clients mentioned their disability and focussed on it in the interview, because it was uppermost in their minds – thus convincing the potential employer that the person did not think he or she was competent to do the job.

We had to train our clients in techniques that would emphasise their positives first, and that they should mention their disabilities only if they were offered the job.

One woman we employed did exactly that when we interviewed her for a job; she told us afterwards how scared she was that if she told us she had rheumatoid arthritis, we would turn her down. Instead, we talked at length about what this might mean in terms of the requirements of the job, and adjusted her workload accordingly. She became one of our finest basic-skills teachers.

<hr>

One of the best ways we found to encourage people with mental health issues was to get them working outdoors. The sort of projects we created involved clearing a school nature reserve and pond of weeds and rubbish, tidying two churchyards, painting at a community centre, regular gardening in private houses, and – for the youngest group of clients – working doing restoration work at a heritage centre mill. For most, it was a completely new experience, as was getting dirty and manual labour. It seemed particularly suited to those with mental health issues.

<hr>

Every year we had a special day when the whole group came together for joint activities, such as a sports day, indoor Olympics, a walk in the nearby Peak District, a visit to a tram museum or a day at Whitby – some clients had never seen the sea. These days were very much appreciated.

<hr>

Teaching adults to learn to read, write and do sums was a very skilled job that was carried out by our trained staff. I was amused by the inventive ways that ideas were put across.

One day in a teaching session that John took because the regular trainer was away, he showed the group a piece of paper and asked them how much it weighed.

"Nothing," came a chorus of replies.

He then dropped a ream of paper on the table top and said, "Well, how much does that weigh?"

The penny dropped, as they say. He went on to tell them that, as a company, we were planning to expand onto another floor and, in order to decide on how much space to rent, we needed to have some idea of the area of each room we used currently. "How can we find that?" he asked.

"We could get a measure and go around each room," one said.

"The furniture is in the way," explained another.

"Think smaller," John suggested.

They looked at the floor, which was covered in carpet tiles, and decided consequently to measure one tile, count them along each of two sides of each room (which were joined at a corner), and multiply the two counts to get the total area. Eureka! Chaos ensued as twenty or so clients, each carrying a clipboard, invaded every training room and crawled around the room counting tiles. We had not warned the staff, so we had some quick explaining to do at the end of the day.

Later in the week, we had a staff training day and we asked our team to design the new training suite on the lower floor, which we planned to hire. We gave them some headings to work from, and – leaving aside the idea for a 'jacuzzi suite' – they came up with very helpful ideas.

One day, we got news that the advisers at the jobcentres were going to carry out an assessment of clients' literacy and numeracy skills during their twenty-minute interview before they referred them on. We were horrified at this news, since we knew that such an assessment needs to be done by skilled people over a period of time. We were asked to give the jobcentre advisers some idea of how it could be done.

I went to a jobcentre, and about two dozen advisers from jobcentres across the city were sitting and waiting for me. I wanted to give them some awareness of how it felt for the client to be asked by a stranger to do a test on reading and spelling in a few minutes, which that client had failed at in all of their school years. So, I started by saying that I was going to begin with giving them a spelling test. The looks of horror on their faces was quite amusing. They were very anxious about the test and all wanted to know how well they had done. Only one person got every spelling correct.

I said to them, "You have just experienced a little of the fear your clients feel when you ask them to do a test."

Following this training, we got the contract to deliver the assessments at the jobcentres ourselves. Once again, I was aware of having to teach about disability and disadvantages to those who should know.

One day, a young woman arrived for an assessment with me. The purpose of the process, which was rigorous and lasted about an hour, was to enable me to see whether we could help a potential client. We talked together about a whole range of issues to do with life and work experiences in order to create a written plan of action. C, the client, had an English degree from Cambridge University. She had trained subsequently to be a librarian, but had worked for local government. She described bullying behaviour by a male superior over a period of time. She had complained to a senior person and was asked to leave.

When I first saw her, she was extremely nervous and ill at ease. She did not believe we could help her, and she insisted on writing down, word for word, everything I said and questioning my motive for each question. It was hard going. She agreed after a while that a period of time with us to learn a new skill might be helpful, but, like most of our clients, she was adamant that she wanted a job *now*; she needed to be employed for her own self-esteem.

As other staff members at SIW and I got to know her better, we experienced her extreme reactions to everyday things – she was not happy in any situation where she felt the slightest possibility of rejection. With much persuasion, she joined the Women's Group and sat quietly, writing down everything anyone said, to the consternation of the others in the group.

She pressed so hard for an opportunity to work that we placed her with a company in a town a few miles from the city centre. She was adamant that we must take her there every day and collect her to go home. This work placement soon broke down because of her behaviour, and she came to me for a meeting. As I sat down, she broke into a very angry tirade against all of us who had not yet found her a job. I sat and listened – though feeling under some threat – until she quietened down, and then I suggested that our observations had led us to believe she was not ready for work, but needed to seek medical advice. I told her we could not continue to work with her as her health seemed to be holding her back. This made her extremely agitated and upset – resulting in a colleague, on hearing her shouting, pushing the panic button! Eventually, she calmed down, and I said we would not see her again until she had seen her doctor. She was diagnosed subsequently with paranoid delusions and received treatment.

Many months later, she phoned me and asked if I would see her again, which of course I did. She was much better in health and more stable emotionally, and we were able to place her for some limited work experience as a receptionist at a beauty parlour, just to give her some contact with the general public. In due course, she gained employment at the large city hospital, working with the Patient Advice and Liaison Service (PALS) team, offering support to patients going to clinics, etc. and is – to my knowledge – still there many years later. Her insights into her own problems had helped her think differently about satisfactory work.

When, we finally discharged her from our list, she wrote a very moving letter to the employment service, identifying all the help we had given her over the two years it took to get her back into work. The employment advisers were impressed, but realised that much of that time spent by our team was unpaid, since we had to work to a contract with the same limited time constraints as those helping able, job-ready graduates, which was always a gripe with us. It was never possible to convince the authorities of these issues, yet they looked to us to find work for the most difficult and challenging people.

Another client, J, came out of a nursing career with a back injury. After some time with us, she wrote this poem:

Physically I was 'disabled'
But when I came to you
It was my heart and my head
That needed a 'wheelchair'
You provided that 'wheelchair'

You nurtured, supported, encouraged
When I fell back you caught me
You gave me back my pride
My self-esteem, my self-respect

When I arrived, my confidence
Was in my boots
Now it is head high
You have given me a fighting chance
For that I will be eternally grateful
Forever in your debt
You hugged me and held me
All of the way
Now I take my first independent steps
Thank you

Here is my hug for you! J

One day, at the end of a session leading the Women's Group, a client asked to see me in private. She said to me, "There's a new person in the group today. I know her."

"Oh! Is she a friend?" I enquired.

"She's my daughter. I haven't spoken to her for over twenty years." There was a pause. She looked tearful and continued, "My husband died very suddenly of a brain tumour, and she blamed me for his death. She never got over it."

"What do you want to do? She has a right to be here and in the group too."

"I don't know. I would like to speak to her, but I don't think I can; there was so much anger."

I had a silent 'prayer for guidance' moment and said, "Would you like me to speak to her?"

"I think I would."

Later that day, I sought out her daughter.

"I know what you are going to say," she stated before I spoke. "It's about my mother, isn't it?"

"Yes. She told me about your dad. She would like to talk to you, but is not sure how you would feel," I explained.

"I did blame her. I was very close to my dad and didn't have an opportunity to say goodbye to him when he died. She didn't let me have anything of his – I have not even got a photograph of him. I think I would like to talk to her, but I don't know what to say to her."

"I could sit in with you both and be referee if it gets difficult," I said.

The offer was accepted by both of them, and we met together in private. They sat with their heads down, not facing each other. The atmosphere was tense.

My prayer was answered, and I found myself saying, "It seems to me ladies that all that separates you now is a hug."

They hugged each other, and sobbed long and hard.

Composing herself eventually, the mother reached into her bag and drew out a battered photograph of her dead husband. She said to her daughter, "This is for you. I've carried it around for twenty years, but now it's yours."

They became the best of friends, and were often seen out and about together, looking very happy. Those were some of the golden moments in our work, and, yes, I cried too!

⁂

One summer, there was another such golden moment. Following an inspection of our company, we were invited to a champagne reception in the Royal Society of Arts building in London to hear an address given by David Sherlock, chief inspector of the Training Standards Council, who was speaking to an audience of successful training organisations, including SIW, which had all gained 'outstanding' inspection reports during the previous year.

He said, "At a recent conference, someone came up to me to tell me how good their inspection had been for helping them to improve, and how open and warmly forthright the lead inspector had been. Her response was, 'Their work with disabled people was superb; it was a privilege to see it.' That company was Support Into Work. I am delighted to welcome the company's owners here today."

Wow! I nearly fell off my chair! We were sitting next to representatives of major national companies, such as Monarch Airlines, who didn't get a mention. Just as delighted were our team of advisers and clients back at SIW.

This had been our first experience of an inspection, and we had been understandably nervous, since our future contracts depended on a good outcome. The process required us, as a whole company, to assess our strengths and weaknesses, and to give ourselves grades for each of several areas – grade1 being outstanding through to grade 5, which might close us down! We achieved grade 1 throughout, much to our relief. When the inspectors received our assessment documents prior to starting the inspection they were very sceptical about our opinions of our achievements. The outcome was all the sweeter! As a thank you to our team we organised a trip to London, with a ride on the London Eye.

The staff we employed to work with such a variety of disabled people were chosen very carefully. By 1999, over fifty percent of our employed advisers had a disability and had first come to us as clients needing training to get back into work. We were able to see them in action in training sessions and judge how suited they were to the work. They were a great team. We had an enormous amount of mutual regard for each person's ability to cope with their lot and get on with life. Here are just a few of SIW's stars.

J, a young man who was using a wheelchair because he had spina bifida, came to SIW for help to find a job. He was bright, funny, articulate and a quick learner, but, more importantly, he had the ability to get alongside others and teach them. He dismissed his own difficulties with humour and encouraged others to do the same; he was a really inspiring person and a great role model for those who felt they could not get work with a disability.

He became a qualified assessor and stayed with the company throughout its existence; he became a firm friend. Our External Assessor had to review his work and was always full of praise for his excellent records. He liked to go 'clubbing' at weekends with his mates. He told me that if he arrived on his own and there were stairs, he would ask any passer-by to give him a lift up! He was never left out in the cold.

C, a basic-skills trainer, came to us feeling very low. She was suffering with her health and with very poor self-esteem. She also had fibromyalgia, so we spoke a common language about our limitations.

She said she had only been a dinner lady and did not feel adequate to be a trainer alongside all the people around her. We helped her to get NVQ qualifications and basic-skills expertise, and she became an excellent worker with the young disabled learners and those with the most severe problems. The learners all expressed their love and respect for her no-nonsense approach – with lots of kindness as a back-up.

J, a very talented and experienced trainer, came to us in 2001 for an interview for a job as a basic-skills teacher. Three years later, she wrote to me:

> At the end of the interview I told Anita and John that I had Rheumatoid Arthritis. I had spent a great deal of time debating how I would explain this. I had developed the condition fairly recently and I was trying to come to terms with it myself. I did feel that it could adversely affect my chances of getting the job. As it transpired I had not understood the ethos and philosophy of the company, which is SIW. I gradually realised that several members of staff had various conditions and disabilities, and that these difficulties were not only encompassed, but handled with such knowledge and understanding that it was clear that people were valued for their abilities and that is what was built on. Allowing staff to maintain dignity and respect was paramount.
>
> I was never put in a position where I had to apologise or was made to feel inadequate for being unable to complete a task – we all understood where any difficulties lay and this was accepted and worked with.
>
> Everyone involved in Support Into Work supported each other, both staff and clients. This is simply what we did. We worked with clients who not only had physical disabilities and health problems, but also many social problems, involving anything from lack of self-esteem, personal hygiene problems, addiction to alcohol, drugs or glue, to housing problems.

Counselling was offered together with contacts with all outside agencies to support people in every way. Part of the training was not only to encompass these difficulties but to actively work with people to help alleviate them and enable the development of life skills, job opportunities and realisation of potential.

I have gained an immeasurable amount of understanding of the difficulties which some people have to live through, and how to recognise, value and build on abilities. I have also learned, because of the hard work the staff applied to their roles, the joy of the individual person's self-recognition and progress.

She was a very special teacher who could inspire those with the most difficulties and help them forward. She was always modest and unsure about her own capabilities, despite all the evidence before her. She is still a much-valued friend.

This is from a press release about another client:

T has a job – it's the one he dreamed of – the one he never imagined he would achieve.

After leaving the army T had a varied career in jobs that required a range of physical strengths and skills. In his mid 30's with a wife and three young children, he was struck down resulting in partial paralysis. He has had to use a wheelchair since then. He came to SIW for help in 1999, and through training and support from all the team began to be less angry about his seemingly hopeless situation and was persuaded to pursue his dream. To this end he studied and worked hard to achieve qualifications in information technology.

The chance of a work placement with a Derby based company was the key. The Managers were most supportive of giving him a chance early in 2000 to prove he could work in their overhead line design engineering section. T in turn worked very hard to demonstrate his skills. The company gave him a project to 'get his teeth into' and he rewarded them with a good outcome.

Soon T, with the support of advisers from SIW was able to discuss real paid work with the company.

Today we are celebrating the signing of his contract – well done! And well done to the engineering company for giving a young man the chance to prove his abilities and bringing him back into the world of employment, work mates and wages.

The human story behind his success was interesting. He was a very angry young man when we first saw him. He felt he had not been supported by the army since he had become disabled. He revealed that he was having difficulties at home because of his anger. One of our advisers was able to persuade him to try an organisation offering anger-management courses. He joined one of the courses, stuck with it and transformed his life.

As he left for full-time employment, his wife came to tell us that his time with us had rescued the whole family; she declared, "I've got my husband back."

CHAPTER THIRTY-FOUR

The New Deal

In 1997, the Department for Employment Service rolled out a national programme for training and support for eighteen- to twenty-five-year-olds called New Deal. This group of young people were finding it especially hard to find work without a lot of support. The government put vast amounts of money into training special employment advisers and upgrading jobcentres, using a bright-orange colour, where these young people would be interviewed and referred for training. SIW gained a contract to help youngsters in this age group who had a range of difficulties preventing them from finding employment on their own. The young people had a variety of problems. Some had a physically limiting disability. Some had been bullied badly at school and lacked confidence to seek work. Many had problems with reading, writing and numbers. Some had significant learning problems. We agreed to take anyone referred to us without realising fully the extent of the problems we were taking on.

This was a new departure for us. John had been the head of a secondary school for a number of years in his past career. I had many years of teaching children and teenagers with all kinds of disabilities, and of finding work placements for some of the older pupils in my school. The rest of our team had no experience of this age group, and there were some anxieties about managing young people who might not be able to cope with our structured learning environment, since they would have to mix with many much older clients in activities such as computing. The prospect of bad behaviour from disaffected youths was a concern also.

I decided to lead a programme to develop their communication skills, based around a series of practical group tasks that would help them identify their interests and abilities. The individual clients had a wide range of conditions and baggage – in the same way that most of our older clients had. It was clear to me that sitting at desks all day being lectured at was the last thing they needed. Gradually, I devised and refined a series of fun activities that captured their imaginations, and drew them in to being more confident, assertive and self-critical. At first, the word 'game' would elicit a groan and blank looks! I tried to relate what they were doing to real situations in the workplace.

Early in the programme we discussed rules at work, since some of them clearly did not see why they should follow what was to them 'meaningless' rules. We began with rules in the training rooms, and they quickly decided that bad language and using a phone was off limits during training. In this way, they developed and guided the group's thinking on what was acceptable. They insisted on having a written list of rules, which they held each other to account for. I sent them around our training rooms to look for rules, and we debated the point of them. Gradually, they began to see their own responsibilities in the workplace and became a much more joined-up group. I only accepted positive feedback from them.

After a time, whenever I entered the classroom at the beginning of a training session one of them would ask, "What game are we playing today?"

One early task was for them to identify, from cards I provided, a set of personal skills and qualities that they felt matched themselves. The list might contain such words and phrases as friendly, helpful, positive, careful, tidy, good with numbers, can spell, etc. Then they would elicit from each member of their small group of four or five people any other personality traits that had been observed. They were only allowed to be positive. After each person had written a long list of identified characteristics, I asked each of them to write at the top of the list, "I am…".

Finally, each of them, in turn, had to read their list out loud to the group. This last task was extremely difficult for them to do, as they had no experience of being asked to acknowledge their good points to others, but it was very rewarding when they did it. They, of course, gained a huge amount of self-esteem from hearing and reading what the others thought of them, and it helped the group to gel and to support each other in their further training.

I was always delighted to work with this group, as – although some of them could be challenging – they always made great progress and friendships.

One young man, another J, was inclined to talk non-stop in sessions. One day, I suggested that if he thought he could do my job he should come out to the front of the class.

Without hesitation he strode up to me, took a marker pen from me and turned to the board. He made a large dot on the paper, turned to the class and said, "First bullet point!" then he sat down and did not speak again.

Another morning, he disappeared from the training centre. John was alerted and asked that the young man should see him when he returned. Much later, J appeared.

"Where have you been?" asked John.

"I've been for an interview for a job," was J's reply.

"What job?"

"A job at B&Q at Spondon."

John, knowing that none of our trainers had sent him for interview responded, "Well, I have to go out; I will take you there and see how you got on."

John and J got into the car and travelled to the store on the outskirts of the city.

On arriving in the car park, John asked, "Is this the store?"

"No, it's down the road," confirmed J.

They drove some considerable way and J said finally, "Turn right, down there."

This was a country lane. John did as he was instructed, and they soon reached a gate to a field.

John announced, "This is not true, is it? You are just telling me lies."

"Yes," replied J.

He was fond of making up stories and tried to convince other clients that he was the UK's secretary for the ABBA Fan Club! It was this detachment from reality that prevented us from helping him to move forward.

———⊸∘⊷———

D was another young man with a mission. He had significant learning difficulties and had no idea what kind of work he could do. We got him some work experience, for which he needed to get a passport photo so the employer could make a badge for him. I agreed to take him into the town to a photo booth.

On the way, he became very animated and told me that what he really wanted was a girlfriend. He asked me how he could get one. I told him he had to meet someone whom he liked, get to know her and then ask her for a date.

We arrived at the shopping centre, parked the car and went inside, where we waited in a queue at the photo booth.

A young woman walked past, and D enquired, "She's nice, shall I ask her now?" as he moved to go after her.

It was hard to explain the normal rules of courtship that would certainly apply in his family.

———⊸∘⊷———

Romance was often in the air, since many of these youngsters did not have opportunities to mix with other young people outside of their homes. One young couple got engaged during the lunch break one day; a ring was bought at the market. They were very close and insisted on being in the same training sessions at all times. The young lady had significant learning difficulties, but was clearly very much in love and talked about their wedding plans. The relationship thrived until Christmas came around.

We always held a party for all our trainees at Christmas time, and, no matter what their faith, they all joined in with great enthusiasm. One of our advisers warned me that trouble was expected between the two lovebirds. During the games session, there was a call for hush. The young fiancé went across to his girlfriend, demanded to have the ring back (she duly obliged), crossed the room, and on bended knee proposed to another girl and put the ring on her finger! The distress and embarrassment was enormous, the fall out continued, but the second engagement produced a baby and a marriage in due course, and they are still together!

An ex-colleague, J, wrote to me about this couple some years later; she explained:

> Some of my most memorable clients were [S] and [G]. I assessed [S] on his level 1 Business Admin NVQ. He met [G] another client at SIW and they had a baby. A few years ago I bumped into [S] at the Royal Hospital where he was working as a porter and really enjoying it. The baby is now a teenager and he and [G] are still together.
>
> We could not have guessed that their relationship would last.
>
> The thing I remember most about these clients was their lack of confidence and self-worth, and with help and support from different staff in different ways they went on to greater things which personally, for me as a new Assessor[,] helped me to think I was doing it right. I think how grateful I was for the opportunity

to use and develop my existing skills and then train and work as an assessor – I am still using those skills today.

Working at SIW was the best job I ever had, the work environment and talented colleagues were some of the best and nicest I have ever worked with[,] and I always felt lucky to enjoy my job and I have never taken a job for granted. I remember John saying to me once how important it was to develop skills, experience and qualifications others don't have as it can put you ahead of others in different situations.

This young man came to SIW as a client, having lost a job and been overworked by an uncaring employer. As a wheelchair user with spina bifida, he had enormous obstacles to overcome in the workplace, but he never complained or sought any special treatment. He trained with us as a client, we employed him as an NVQ assessor and the area manager of NVQ qualifications identified him as one of the most successful assessors he had ever seen.

—∞—

Not every aspect of training was always successful. There were some, naturally, for whom this active-participation style of learning was not acceptable. We had to be inventive in finding ways of reaching shy, frightened people. Sometimes, getting them to befriend a client with greater physical needs was a way forward. Some of our older clients were extremely good at this kind of support and benefited as much from it as the young person they helped.

—∞—

We had a visit one day from a civil servant from the Department for Work and Pensions. Word had got out from clients talking at the jobcentres about how excellent and different our training was. He arrived in immaculate pinstriped suit. John, after discussing figures and targets with him, suggested that he might like to sit in on one of my training sessions with the young people, and he agreed somewhat reluctantly. I invited him to join in the session, but he declined; it was usually my policy that if someone came into my training sessions to see what we did, they had to join in – if only to experience how it felt to be a newcomer speaking to strangers.

Our session was a practical debate on current topics – the first being smoking. I asked each participant to stand next to a statement about smoking that reflected their own viewpoint. Next, they each in turn had to justify their viewpoint to someone in an opposing group. This led to much lively discussion, and the session went well – in my view.

At the end of the session, the visitor thanked me curtly, returned to see John in his office and said, "I have no idea what was happening in there but they all seemed to enjoy it."

He did not have the imagination to see how valuable it was for the young people to speak out, to argue constructively, to stick with their own opinion, or be able to change it without losing face, etc. All of which are good strategies for talking about themselves successfully at interviews.

One day, I set up my painting easel, paints, etc. and invited the group into the room without saying anything. I asked them to talk together about their hobbies. They were all uncharacteristically quiet.

After a while, I got their attention, as I picked up a paint brush, and told them that I had always wanted to learn to paint and had just now enrolled on a course on watercolour painting.

A young man's hand went up. "So, we don't have to learn to paint then, Anita?" he said with relief in his voice.

That was the reason for the subdued atmosphere when had they first arrived. I told them how difficult it was to learn a new skill and how my first results were rubbish. I showed them my cringeworthy first landscape, and they were very kind and positive – and encouraged me to keep on trying to get better. Eventually, I was asked to set up a drawing and painting class for clients who wanted to have a go. Me, teaching art when I was a complete novice myself!

Around that time, John and I had joined one of our sons on a trip to Oslo, where we saw the painting by Munch called *The Scream*. I bought a postcard, studied it and realised it was composed of a series of lines. I gave copies to my art group, told them to turn the picture upside down and draw the lines as they saw them. Their results astonished them and me. They were encouraged greatly by believing that they could produce a work of art. Regularly, many of their pictures were hung around the corridors and meeting rooms of the centre and were admired by all.

By these varied means their confidence grew, and their ability to speak out about themselves improved.

We had a superb woman who came to ask if she could volunteer to teach our women clients how to embellish and make their own clothes. In weekly sessions, she did some amazing work – turning jeans into skirts and bags, and embellishing sweaters and jeans with motifs – and she took the clients to local markets and charity shops to buy the clothes cheaply.

I told the clients one day that I wanted each of them to prepare a five-minute speech to be given to the group about their hobby during the next session. They found this very daunting, but – with some help from our adult volunteers – they came up with some amazing hobbies, such as pigeon racing and fishing. Each individual's knowledge of their own hobby was impressive, and I was able to put those skills to good use in future training.

The feedback from the rest of the group was always positive, as they had learned to support each other in any difficult situation. As often as we could, we arranged for the clients to undertake activities out in the community. I once asked this group of young people to carry out a survey of all the buildings that had once been cinemas in the city centre – there were a lot, and the resulting histories were interesting to everybody.

The clients decided they needed a weekly newssheet to let everybody know what was going on within the company. I had a number of complaints from individuals who heard that others had been out on an interesting trip that they wanted to go on too. Sometimes it felt like being back at school teaching! The resulting newssheets were surprising. They were produced in colour, and their production was assisted by older volunteers from the computer training sessions. The content included bulletins on activities, an interview with a member of staff and clients' success stories.

⸙

We had some very good successes in finding employment for this age group – so much so that the jobcentre advisers began to ask John to talk to other companies about how we did it. This is not the sort of thing that commercial companies are keen to do. However, we had an insight in that other companies would not value nor be prepared to work with young people in the ways we did to gain results, especially as this kind of work was not funded by the employment service. We had to seek funds through European Projects to be able to do so. So, we were open in describing our activities, but, of course, without motivated and skilled staff, it would not work.

Other organisations in conversation with John would state that they did all that anyway, which they clearly didn't. Or they would say it was a waste of time and they did not get paid to play games. There was little understanding about the philosophy behind such work.

We were required by the employment service to provide training and work experience for thirty hours a week. Most large training companies would get their clients out into a workplace as quickly as possible – so that they did not have to train them in-house, and they could then take in many more clients for a fee up front. We could not work this way, even if it had been the right thing to do, because our clients had to have a considerable period of in-house training to prepare them for the workplace. Keeping everyone motivated for thirty hours a week was a challenge, especially when a considerable number of clients could not read and write – and, later, we had many who could not speak English. However, we enabled our clients to gain a sense of self-worth, dignity and a purpose in life. The successes were certainly worth the hard work.

We became part of a European-funded project in which we were twinned with a group in Italy to look at employment for disabled young people, because of our successful reputation in this work.

At the end of the first year, a colleague and I travelled to Foggia, on the heel of Italy, for a conference. John could not go, so J – our disabled receptionist, who was a wheelchair user – joined me on the trip. We flew from East Midlands Airport to Naples and then travelled by train to Foggia; it was a very gruelling day for both of us.

When we arrived, we were whisked away – without any explanation – to a large shopping centre. At the shopping centre, a crowd of people stood around a Christmas tree, with the local mayor in full regalia at the front. There were long speeches – in Italian – and lots of clapping and cheering. We had no idea what was going on. My colleague J was given a doll to keep her quiet; the assumption being that people in wheelchairs are all childlike.

J, who was a registered nurse of many years' experience, looked at me and said, "Don't breathe a word about this back at work!"

But, of course, I did!

The rest of the weekend was more positive. The next day, we were taken to watch a swimming gala at a school for disabled children and to a horticultural project where young people worked in greenhouses. Discussion about 'real work' for these young people was difficult: their parents felt it would be too risky, and that employers would not want to employ disabled people.

In addition, we got to sample superb local cuisine: lots of pasta, shellfish and meats, which made the trip more worthwhile. Plus, we were in a beautiful part of Italy.

During 2001, John and I became involved with a small team of consultants employed by the government to deliver training programmes to other companies around the UK. The government was about to introduce inspections for training companies such as those carried out by Office for Standards in Education, Children's Services and Skills (Ofsted) in schools.

Our role was to design and introduce a format for the assessment of the clients' learning and progress that could be used across all training companies. This was to be a whole new way of working and recording activities with learners.

The new mantra was to be "Put the learner at the centre of everything you do." For us, this fitted well with the way we worked. For other large companies it was completely against the ways they worked and would require a big change in their practices, including retraining staff. So, it was sometimes a difficult message to put over.

We travelled to most of the big cities, from Edinburgh to Cardiff to London, over a period of eight years, and met a lot of people working in our sector. The big surprise to us was how poor some large companies were at delivering appropriate programmes for learners with any kind of disadvantage or disability; their focus was profit as the bottom line in most cases. We did get valuable insights into how the system of assessment for performance worked – just as Ofsted was beginning to be involved in adult training. This consultancy activity was in addition to managing SIW, which was very successful at this time, and employed thirty people.

At home, our family began to grow. In 2009, we had a happy day accompanying my eldest son Shaun, Jannette, his fiancée and her infant son Dylan to an adoption hearing, at which Dylan was adopted formally by Shaun. It was a wonderful experience, and Dylan beamed every time he heard his name mentioned in the social report to the magistrates, who were wonderful to him and to us as a family. We all shed a tear, except Dylan, who presented his dad with a chocolate badge for 'Best Dad in the World' before getting his reward – a new bike. We had champagne in a café by the sea and felt truly overjoyed.

Shaun and Dylan have always had a close relationship, and this was just the icing on the cake. Jannette has been a great partner to Shaun, and we feel very close to them both. We spend time looking after Dylan in the summer holidays and he always entertains us.

John and I have been fortunate in that we have travelled to a number of countries since we retired. After several holidays in the Algarve, we decided to purchase an apartment there. In 2006, we acquired a holiday home in a quiet area of Vilamoura, and have enjoyed many happy times there with family and a growing number of friends whom we have met, and continue to meet, through our local church.

When my son David visited our apartment in Portugal later that spring, he spent a lot of time on his mobile. Gradually, he revealed that he had met someone.

"Is she *the one*, Dave?" I asked.

"Could be," was all he said then, but later in the week he declared, "I must bring Alison here, Mum."

When we met Alison, we knew instinctively that they were right for each other. She is a truly lovely person, and we love her very dearly – and she is a teacher! They were married in June 2011 on a beautiful island off the coast of Zakynthos. I felt the mixed emotions of happiness and sadness felt by all mothers on seeing a much-loved son getting married.

During his speech at the wedding breakfast, he revealed a secret. He and Alison had met through internet dating – as his brother and Jannette had too. Dave's best man, Rick, embellished the tale by saying that when they shared a house whilst Dave studied for his PhD, he would spend all day in his room on his computer studying, only appearing at 5pm to ask Rick, "What's for tea?"

"Except one day, Dave appeared through the front door with this beautiful blonde on his arm," Rick continued.

I thought, *How did that happen?* Now we knew!

Dave and Alison now have two lovely boys – William, who was born in 2012, and Nathaniel, who was born in 2014 – and we are so proud of them both.

John's eldest son, Phil married Lynda in 2007, and they have a daughter, Abigail who is bright, entertaining and has lots of friends. We love to spend time with all of them.

It has been one of my life's greatest joys to be a grandmother. In our apartment in Ashbourne, I keep a wooden chest full of toys and games for my grandchildren. Without exception they each dive into this chest as soon as they enter the door. I have to remember to renew the toys with surprises appropriate to their interests as they grow.

I am so grateful for the experience I have had with my mothers-in-law, who have each showed me how to entertain and amuse the little ones, and to how be a good grandmother.

Getting back to my work, by 2011 and despite our success with the most disadvantaged people, we heard that the government had decided only to contract nationally with large organisations on the basis that 'big is better'. We were encouraged to join up with the chosen companies. When these contracts started, we found those same companies did not honour their commitment to us and we were soon without clients.

Sadly, we had to close SIW, making fifteen of our loyal staff redundant. It was a very dark time and left us reeling. It was sad to hear that, within months, our former clients were receiving no help and the government was asking where all the expertise had gone!

We heard an awful new term 'parking and creaming', which referred to a company's procedure of seeing many new clients, carrying out an interview and selecting only those who were near to getting a job, so that income came in quickly. It was said that disadvantaged people were left at home with an occasional phone call to check if they had got a job, which could bring a fee to the training company. What a contrast to all the support we had given to every one of our clients. We were appalled.

When, finally, I retired from SIW in 2006 – tired and not well – it took me some time to adjust. I was glad to be free of the routine, the hard work, and the long days managing my fatigue and pain.

Strangely, memories of difficult events in my past life began to occur. I would often wake up in the night after bad dreams, sweating and fearful, with my heart racing and my mouth dry. I felt an overwhelming sense of guilt about things I had done wrong in my life, people I had hurt and people who had hurt me. I often felt very angry and was not easy to live with. I tried hard not to dwell on these dark thoughts and to fill my time with new things to do. I started watercolour painting with some success; I tried yoga, but was too exhausted to continue; and I found a great young teacher to restart me on my cello playing. My husband helped me chose a new car – a Honda MX5 – and I enjoyed bombing about the country lanes in it! It was a time of freedom and a new more relaxed pace.

Whenever I met up with friends and old colleagues from my past, they would invariably say to me something like, "Do you remember so and so? You should write a book!"

Gradually, after I retired, the idea began to appeal to me. It could be a legacy for my children and grandchildren to know about our history. So I began.

CHAPTER THIRTY-FIVE

Venes Family Reunited

DURING THE EARLY YEARS OF MY RETIREMENT, I HAD regular contact with my sister and her family. We had reached a good understanding about our lives and our losses, though she continued to feel angry about her past.

When she heard about my book and read an early transcript, she said to me, "I would like to find out what happened to me. I want to know where I got sent to and why."

I encouraged her to contact The Children's Society, as I had done many years before, to ask them for details from her records, which they must still have. Eventually, she did so, and meetings were arranged with a social worker.

There followed a period of several months of visits, uncovering lots of very painful issues for Sandra. She said at times she thought she would never come through the awful emotions she experienced in reading her history and remembering some of it. I was shocked to hear that she had been in ten different homes before the age of seven. The relationship with her social worker was a very positive and caring one, and Sandra began gradually to put her life in place and to feel less upset.

During that time the social worker asked Sandra if she would like to find out about our brother, Graham. Sandra talked to me, and I agreed, but did not hold out much hope of finding him after such a long time.

However, I got a call from my sister a few days later; she asked, "Anita, are you sitting down?"

Knowing she was at the hospital that morning, I panicked and replied:

"Why? What's the matter? Are you OK?"

"Yes, fine. I had a call from the social worker, A, this morning. She has found our brother Graham!"

It seemed The Children's Society had found a match to his last known whereabouts and had contacted him to be sure he was our brother. In a letter to him, the social worker had said that his birth sisters were enquiring about him and asked if he would like to be put in contact with us.

Sandra continued, the social worker, A, said that when she rang him it was extremely emotional. Graham cried a lot, and said he was overjoyed to hear he had a family. He had wondered all his life about his birth family."

We talked and decided we would risk a phone call – he might be any sort of rogue for all we knew!

When Dawn, my niece, discovered my father's history online, I had encouraged my sister to join me in meeting our dad's second family to learn about our dad's life. She was very against this and said she felt cheated knowing that he had gone on to create another family and lived 'happily ever after', whilst we little children were going through so much and living apart. However, I wanted to know more about him.

By 2015, I had persuaded Sandra to meet our half-sister Elaine and her husband Mick. Both are lovely, warm, welcoming people, who said they would like to meet Sandra.

On 16th July 2015 two amazing things happened. Sandra came to our home to meet Elaine and Mick for the first time. They and she were delighted to meet up at last, and it was a very happy occasion.

Sandra had also agreed to have a conversation with Graham that day. We rang him whilst we were all together and had the phone on conference mode, so we could all hear his voice. It was a very joyful but emotional conversation. Graham had no idea that he had two sisters, and there was much talking over each other trying to help him work out who was whom in our extended families.

Graham's story was that he was adopted soon after birth and joined a kind, caring couple. Sadly, his father died when he was just nine, and his mother sank into depression, never recovering from her loss. He left school at fourteen and started work on a farm in order to support his mother. The death of his father, together with his mother's ill health, led him to long to know about the supposedly happy birth family from which he had been banished.

Arrangements were made to meet Graham and his wife Pat who live in Chippenham in Wiltshire, the following week.

We all arrived together at Sandra's house. We sat in her garden for photographs and Graham's endless joking made us cry with laughter. He was very entertaining and it was such a wonderful day for us all, but especially for him. Pat scribbled furiously in a notebook, trying to record who all our family members were. There were a lifetime's worth of stories to be shared. Sandra was overjoyed about meeting him, and the event made up for all the difficult memories dredged up by her reading her own records.

Graham's life has been very colourful and eventful; he is one of life's special characters, and we have found an immediate bond with him and Pat. During his varied work life, he has held several jobs. He worked in a garage, then he joined a business doing stonework repairs on churches and old buildings. Gradually, he developed a skill for carving stone. He showed us photographs of some amazing stone carving that was his work. He is clearly gifted with his hands.

Graham became disappointed with how little he earned, so he left this work to join a circus in 1979. He worked with a number of circuses, and built up a reputation as a clown and illusionist. In talking to him, I realised that he had been with a circus in our home town in the 1990s, to which we had taken two of our children! It is sad to think that if Graham and I had come face to face, then we would not have recognised each other. Ultimately, Graham's circus career took him all over the world and he became 'Potts', international circus clown and mime artist, appearing on *Blue Peter* and many other television programmes. His publicity brochure describes him as this:

The face to launch (or is it sink) a thousand ships.
A unique mime artist with the most expressive face and body language combining to tell a story without words.

Even when he is trying to be inconspicuous, people stop and laugh at his antics.

He will make the young and old alike cry with tears of laughter at his own misfortune.

This shy, bashful, helpless character is loved by all who see him.

Potts could have stepped out of the television series, 'Allo 'Allo! with the outrageous French accent, onions, map and bike all helping to tell a story.

As Potts, Graham toured with both English and French circuses, and also spent a season with the stars from the Bulgarian State Circus. He has been a frequent street performer, both on stilts and fire-eating. He represented England at Expo '92 in Seville and has appeared in Holland, the Middle East and at the Dubai Tennis Open – as the warm-up act for Tim Henman and others.

But – sitting in his living room, listening to his stories and watching him 'perform' – I was amazed and delighted to have such an unusual and talented brother. He is totally animated and excited about his life; his wife has to tell him to put his arms down when he is telling a story.

When we reminisce about family, the tears come quickly and he is filled with remorse that he never knew his own mother. It is clear from our records that he was probably not my father's son. His resemblance to our maternal grandfather, however, is uncanny, as is me sitting next to him with our grandma's face. Most families will not find this especially unusual, but it is amazing to us who have never known family. We took Graham a framed photograph of our mum when we went to visit him at his home in Wiltshire. There were tears all round as he said, "I wish I'd known her."

I have struggled with how to make the complex, sad person that our mum was seem real to him. I think the story of her fractured life has been difficult to understand. We have talked a lot about forgiveness and how we cannot judge the circumstances that caused Mum to give away all her children. I don't know how she would have coped if we had all been reunited before she died. There were so many secrets in our young lives.

Graham once said to me, "Look at you, you're so clever. Me, I'm nothing."

I hugged him, told him that was rubbish, and joked about the excitement I am getting from having such a famous, unusual brother in my family. I wish I had known him all my life. I am immensely proud to know him and to learn about his story.

He entertained our grandchildren at my seventieth birthday party, and our grandson William told his teacher the next day, "My grandma had a birthday party, and there was a clown and he did magic tricks!"

His teacher said to Alison, his mum, "You have a very unusual mother-in-law!"

You can say that again!

I was always sad at growing up as an only child in my foster home. Graham's life would have fascinated me certainly, and we could have had some good times together.

In the end, I became part of a family of seven children. How amazing!

Finally, all our family met together at last for a very special party.

Watch this space for my next book about
Graham and his amazing life.